Cultural Heritage Conservation for Early Learners

Cultural Heritage Conservation for Early Learners explores how to introduce young audiences to art conservation. Conservators and educators from around the world share their approach to creating engaging, hands-on programs for children aged three to eight and their caregivers.

Drawing on their experiences as conservators and educators, the authors provide an in-depth look at the Smithsonian Institution's popular "Art & Me" family workshops. Readers will gain practical insights into the workshop design, which draws upon years of program evaluation and discover how these workshops foster an understanding of cultural preservation; familiarize attendees with museum spaces; and encourage a sense of responsibility for preserving history and culture. The book also explores case studies beyond the United States, showcasing diverse approaches to early learner engagement in cultural heritage conservation. These real-world examples, encompassing various settings and collaborations, delve into the adaptation of virtual and online resources in response to contemporary challenges.

Cultural Heritage Conservation for Early Learners is an indispensable guide for emerging and established educators, conservators, and museum professionals who wish to integrate art conservation and cultural heritage preservation into early learning. It is a valuable resource for anyone interested in innovative, arts integration teaching methods that enhance critical thinking and foster a deeper appreciation of cultural heritage.

Ellen Chase is Objects Conservator at the Smithsonian Institution's National Museum of Asian Art, where she has worked toward the long-term preservation of the collection since 1999. Her research interests focus on a range of materials including ceramics and lacquer, as well as investigating ways to bring an appreciation of cultural heritage conservation to diverse audiences. Ellen is active in a range of community outreach and engagement activities both through the museum and as a part of the American Institute for Conservation's Education Outreach (K-12) Subcommittee.

Laura Hoffman specializes in online and visitor engagement. As Director of Digital Engagement at the National Museum of Women in the Arts, she oversees institutional digital initiatives and leads a team responsible for expanding the museum's online presence. In her previous role as Program Manager, she developed public programs, interpretation, and digital engagement for the Lunder Conservation Center at the Smithsonian American Art Museum. Laura has also held digital and education positions at The Phillips Collection and deCordova Sculpture Park and Museum. She has served on various professional committees for the Museum Computer Group and the American Institute for Conservation.

Matthew Lasnoski serves as a Digital Services Analyst in the Taxpayer Experience Office of the Internal Revenue Service. From 2014 to 2022, he held multiple positions at the Smithsonian Institution's National Museum of Asian Art (NMAA), including Manager, Youth & Family Programs and Audience Engagement Strategist. During this time, he co-led the museum's Audience Research Team (ART), focusing on audience research and evaluation. Before joining NMAA, Matthew earned his MPhil in History of Art and Architecture at the University of Cambridge, King's College. His research focused on the impact of manufacturing processes on the development of new decorative techniques in Ayyubid metalwork in the early thirteenth century. Matthew also served as an educator at the Smithsonian American Art Museum, with a focus on distance learning through videoconferencing and webinars.

Conservation in Focus

Conservation in Focus is a new series of short-format books that challenges authors and readers to approach the conservation of heritage from a new angle. The series will include theoretical think pieces, reflections on developments in conservation policy, analysis of paradigm-shifting innovations and compelling case studies that will be of interest to an international readership.

Books published within the series will be authored by a diverse range of authors and editors and should be of interest to academics, researchers, and postgraduate students from the fields of conservation, museum and heritage studies and architecture. Books published in the series will be between 20,000 and 50,000 words in length, which will make them accessible to busy practitioners too.

The following list includes only the most-recent titles to publish within the series. A llst of the full catalogue of titles is available at: Conservation in Focus - Book Series - Routledge & CRC Press

Innovative technology in art conservation
Original appearance, viewer perception
William Wei

Cultural Heritage Conservation for Early Learners
Outreach and Engagement with the Next Generation
Ellen Chase, Laura Hoffman, and Matthew Lasnoski

Cultural Heritage Conservation for Early Learners

Outreach and Engagement with the Next Generation

Ellen Chase, Laura Hoffman, and Matthew Lasnoski

Contributions from:

Aimée Bou Rizk, Claire Cuyaubère, Sabine Kretzschmar, Kathleen Lau, Jenny Mathiasson, Raquel Santos, Colleen Snyder, Renée Stein, and Amelia Youssef

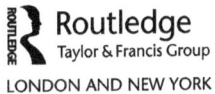
Routledge
Taylor & Francis Group

LONDON AND NEW YORK

First published 2024
by Routledge
4 Park Square, Milton Park, Abingdon, Oxon OX14 4RN

and by Routledge
605 Third Avenue, New York, NY 10158

Routledge is an imprint of the Taylor & Francis Group, an informa business

British Library Cataloguing-in-Publication Data
A catalogue record for this book is available from the British Library

ISBN: 978-1-032-36592-3 (hbk)
ISBN: 978-1-032-36677-7 (pbk)
ISBN: 978-1-003-33321-0 (ebk)

DOI: 10.4324/9781003333210

Typeset in Times New Roman
by KnowledgeWorks Global Ltd.

Contents

Preface

The genesis of this book and the Smithsonian Institution's "Art & Me" program, a conservation outreach program for children aged three to eight and their caregivers, originated with my initial encounter sharing cultural heritage conservation with early learners. Although I had done several outreach programs at middle schools and high schools, it was only when asked to talk with my daughter's preschool class (aged three to four) that I had any experience with conservation-related outreach for young children. While this was just a single visit, I realized that not only were the children receptive to the conservation-focused activities but also seemed to understand the idea of preservation.

From personal experience, I remember little of my early childhood, only a few glimpses here and there, such as the white flecks in my neighbor's red linoleum kitchen floor and the metallic flash of going down the slide at a nearby playground. I do, however, have very distinct and complete memory of the first time I got to finger paint at nursery school (as it was called at the time). I clearly remember my teacher placing the paint on the table in front of me, being able to "smoosh" my hands through the paint and making designs like spaghetti. I also vividly remember my consternation when the teacher said it was time to clean up since I thought my artwork was going to be destroyed in the process, only to be relieved and excited to find that it would be preserved by pressing a sheet of paper on top and making a print of my design. The impulse to preserve things that we care about is innate in humans and that instinct is integral to my memory. I also observed this response in the students when I was working with the preschool class as an adult.

Working with my daughter's class and remembering my own experience sparked an idea and emphasized that when introduced in an appropriate way, cultural heritage preservation outreach is a great opportunity to create a familiarity with the topic to build on as children mature. I was interested in going further with this type of outreach for younger learners, particularly since I found few other conservators who were working with this group on a consistent basis. As was the case with my first exposure, those conservators who had engaged with early learners were asked to take part in a one-time visit to their child's class or alternately had encountered early learners as part of family day programming. None, however, were in an ongoing program focused on the specific needs of this age group.

To develop a program for early learners, I felt that working with an educator familiar with this age group would make the outreach significantly more effective. Although I had put together activities for the early learners in my daughter's class, as an objects conservator, I didn't feel I had the expertise to put together more comprehensive programming that required a more in-depth knowledge of how young children learn and what would be the best way to present the material in an approachable way. Additionally, I was interested in working with the museum's collections, as it would allow a broader approach to programming content since it could incorporate in-gallery experiences and other museum resources. When I reached out to Matthew Lasnoski, the museum's youth & family programs manager, he was interested, and the collaboration began.

Initially, it was difficult to convince some of our colleagues that early learners would benefit from exposure to cultural heritage preservation, but over time the popularity of our program and the related positive feedback began to win people over. Although there are more cultural institutions and individuals working with younger children than when we first started Art & Me in 2016, conservation programming is still mostly limited to outreach for older children. Looking back, I couldn't have envisioned that not only would this program still be going strong after eight years but that other museum professionals, like Laura Hoffman at the Smithsonian Museum of American Art, would enthusiastically work with Matthew and me and to expand the program.

We hope that by sharing our experiences, as well as those from the other case studies included in the book, cultural heritage outreach for early learners will seem less daunting and more feasible both to conservators and educators. The future of cultural heritage is dependent on the next generations and fostering that appreciation and understanding early on are essential components of building that future.

Ellen Chase

Acknowledgments

Writing this book about cultural heritage preservation and early learners has been a multiyear journey that would not have been possible without the support and encouragement of many individuals. From encouraging the development of the Art & Me program to reading draft manuscripts, we are fortunate to have such a remarkable network of people surrounding us.

First and foremost, a commitment like this one would not be possible without the backing of museum leadership. A special thanks goes out to Donna Strahan, Head of Conservation and Scientific Research at the National Museum of Asian Art (NMAA), and Amber Kerr, Head of Conservation at the Lunder Conservation Center at the Smithsonian American Art Museum (SAAM), for their unwavering commitment to this program. A big thank you to both conservation labs, museums, and the Smithsonian Institution as a whole for the ongoing support of intergenerational and early learning.

Over the course of writing this book, we started collaborating closely with Leah Bright, SAAM Objects Conservator. She has played a pivotal role in shaping the Art & Me program as it transitioned to an online format during the COVID-19 pandemic and has sustained the partnership between the two museums as it transitions back to onsite programming. She holds a uniquely important role for the future of the Art & Me program.

In addition, we would like to acknowledge Brooke Rosenblatt, Head of Visitor Experience and Audience Research at NMAA, for her insights on evaluation and programming that greatly improved the final version of this book. Building evaluative capacity, as described in this book, would not have been possible without the mentorship of Andy Pekarik, whose guidance and wisdom is deeply appreciated. Our sincere appreciation extends to NMAA Head of Scholarly Programs and Publications Sana Mirza, whose invaluable institutional knowledge facilitated our administrative approvals to ensure proper progression of all elements within this project.

In our pursuit to gather diverse examples of cultural heritage preservation programming for early learners, we have been immensely fortunate to collaborate with a select group of dedicated case study authors. These case study authors have not only expanded our horizons but have also exemplified the spirit of collaborative scholarship. We extend our heartfelt thanks to Aimée Bou Rizk, Claire Cuyaubère, Sabine Kretzschmar, Kathleen Lau, Jenny Mathiasson, Raquel Santos, Colleen Snyder, Renée Stein, and Amelia Youssef.

We asked multiple individuals to read versions of our book proposal and manuscript, including Ed and Lynann Derrick, Zachary Evans, Maria Iafelice, Lynn Thomson McGowan, and Sarah Rontal. We deeply appreciate their constructive feedback, which was instrumental in refining this work.

We would like to express our gratitude to Heidi Lowther, whose encouragement and support were instrumental in igniting the spark that led to the inception of this book. Additionally, a special thanks to Heeranshi Sharma who guided us through the intricate process leading up to the publication of this book.

Lastly, we would like to acknowledge those who were instrumental in instilling a love of learning at early ages and inspiring us as young children. There are so many family members, friends, teachers, mentors, and community members who have touched our lives in meaningful ways, supporting us now and over the years. We are truly fortunate to have you all in our corner.

1 An Introduction to Cultural Heritage Conservation Outreach for Early Learners

Ellen Chase, Laura Hoffman, and Matthew Lasnoski

Overview

The care and preservation of cultural heritage, whether in museums or elsewhere, has traditionally been out of the public view and sometimes seen as a mysterious or even invisible process. Over time, however, public engagement about conservation practices has become an integral part of the profession. Sharing conservation practice more publicly takes many forms, including museum gallery talks, advocacy days, career days at high schools, and even visible conservation labs where the public can see conservators at work. As the formats of public engagement have broadened, the target audiences and communities have expanded as well. In this book, we explore the unique place early learners occupy within the field of conservation heritage outreach.

To set the stage, this chapter provides details about the current state of public engagement in conservation and shares unique considerations for engaging early learners. Additionally, we address how conservation inherently integrates art and science, making it a natural fit for arts integration and Science, Technology, Engineering, Art, and Mathematics (STEAM)-related educational programming.

In the two succeeding parts of the book, detailed real-world examples illustrate how institutions and individuals develop meaningful conservation outreach programs for early learners. Our hope is that these examples will inspire other practitioners to envision engagement opportunities for early learners by adapting these ideas in their own contexts.

A Look into Conservation-related Public Engagement

The heart of art conservation is preserving cultural heritage, caring for symbols and treasures of communities and societies. Conservation and preservation focus on protecting cultural heritage for the future, including examination, documentation, treatment, and preventive care, supported by research and education (AIC (American Institute for Conservation) n.d.). The International Council of Museums-Committee for Conservation considers conservation to

DOI: 10.4324/9781003333210-1

be "all measures and actions aimed at safeguarding tangible cultural heritage while ensuring its accessibility to present and future generations" (ICOM-CC (International Council of Museums – Committee for Conservation) n.d.). The ideas of scientifically based conservation began in the late 1920s at Harvard University's Fogg Art Museum, with the second such conservation lab in the United States starting at the National Museum of Asian Art in 1951.[1] The field of conservation has evolved over time and now includes consideration of and collaboration with many different stakeholders. As a starting point, conservators follow a code of ethics that guides decisions they make about preserving cultural heritage.[2] These guidelines consider the responsibility of a conservator to the cultural heritage itself, the communities and stakeholders connected to it, and to the profession.

The current state of outreach in the field of cultural heritage preservation can be broken into two distinct contexts: resources and programs produced for the public and those with a more academic focus written for the conservation profession and other museum professionals. A look into each approach provides an enlightening snapshot and insight into the evolving landscape of cultural heritage conservation outreach and engagement.

Overview of Types of Public Engagement in Conservation

Cultural heritage outreach that engages directly with the public exists in a number of forms from in-person programming to online videos. While this book focuses on learning through guided inquiry in formal and informal settings, there are several other ways in which the field has approached engagement with the public, as outreach has become a key component of conservation's mission. Although still relatively uncommon, museums have begun to include dedicated staff for outreach and engagement as part of the conservation department, greatly expanding the availability and depth of cultural heritage conservation programming.

Common forms of conservation-focused public outreach are presentations, gallery talks, and tours because they are cost-effective and popular with adult audiences. These talks and tours often focus on the conservation of a specific artwork or exhibition but can also concentrate on the conservation facilities themselves to give extended access. School career days, field trips, and workshops are offered for younger audiences but are typically for pre-teens, teenagers, and university students. Activity cart and family day programming that include conservation topics recently have started to become more prevalent in museums as an additional way to engage visitors. The structures of carts and family days can allow for more individualized conversations that can be adjusted to the age and learning level of the audience.

Displays devoted to restoration have been around since the eighteenth century; however, exhibitions showcasing conservation and scientific research, whether about a specific project or the field in general, have increased dramatically since the mid-twentieth century (McClure 2013). These exhibitions often focus on the conservation of iconic works, such as the Star-Spangled Banner at the Smithsonian's National Museum of American History or can be more general introductions, such as the conservation galleries at the Ashmolean Museum in Oxford (NMAH n.d., Ashmolean n.d.). In addition to a more traditional format of museum exhibitions, active conservation and research carried out in a gallery setting have become a way to showcase conservation projects to the public. Gallery spaces devoted to the care and preservation of the collection now include long-term set-ups, such as the Conservation in Action gallery at the Museum of Fine Arts Boston, in which conservators and scientists carried out the conservation of numerous works of art over the years before establishing the Conservation Center in 2022 (Museum of Fine Arts Boston 2021). Additionally, labs like the Lunder Conservation Center at the Smithsonian American Art Museum have now become their own permanent gallery space of sorts, providing visual access to the lab for the museum audience (SAAM n.d.).

While exhibitions are often paired with public programming to bolster interpretation, these engagement efforts do not always consider youth audiences as their primary audience. However, signs of change are evident in recent exhibitions, such as the family-focused *Mission Masterpiece* conservation exhibition held at the Rijksmuseum in Amsterdam, which was geared towards children aged eight and older (Rijksmuseum 2023). In a similar vein, *Facelifts and Make-overs* at Mauritshuis in the Netherlands included components for children aged seven and older, including targeted content and design, such as lower vitrines and labels (Meloni and Buvelot 2023). While neither exhibition is specifically for early learners, there are components that are available to them, and these examples are hopefully a starting point for building early learners into future conservation exhibitions.

Additionally, online access to cultural heritage conservation content has increased at an even higher rate over the past decade, particularly with the advent of the COVID-19 pandemic. Many museums and private conservators have at least some level of social media presence, whether it be as an occasional post on a museum account or a dedicated account for a lab or studio. Furthermore, professional organizations have begun to play an active role in social media activities that bring conservation and scientific research to the public, such as the annual "Ask a Conservator Day" organized by the American Institute for Conservation (AIC 2023a). Despite this expanded presence on social media, this content focuses on adults.

Videos, blogs, podcasts, and other online content have also increased dramatically, and videos, in particular, are a medium suited to share resources for early learners. A number of museums have put out lesson plans and videos on their websites but generally they are categorized for elementary, middle, or high school students. For engagement outside of school, videos can be directed towards children, such as the MetKids Microscope series, which is paired with activities and a difficulty level ranging from one to five (Metropolitan Museum of Art n.d.).

With the increase of online public engagement, particularly through social media, video, and museum websites, access to conservation-related content has exploded. Nevertheless, there is a disparity in the quality of these resources. While many in-person events tend to be affiliated with museums and conservation professionals, online viral content about the care and restoration of personal heirlooms can come from unreliable sources without the appropriate training or familiarity with a conservation code of ethics. Unsurprisingly, some of this content can be misleading and inaccurate. For example, a few years ago, there was a story circulated on the internet claiming that one could repair cracks in ceramics by soaking them in warm milk. The theory, presumably, was that the milk protein casein would form a glue that would bond the broken sections of the ceramic together, but this repair process was found to be ineffective, and multiple tests carried out were unsuccessful (Horwitz 2019). Some of these viral suggestions and recommendations can potentially cause extensive and irreversible damage. It is not always easy for the nonprofessional to differentiate the reliability of some of these resources, and as a result, professional organizations such as the Education Outreach (K-12) Subcommittee of the American Institute for Conservation have aggregated resources for educators and families (AIC 2023b).

Moving the Field Forward: Publications on Conservation Outreach

Academic publications provide an opportunity to discuss and critically approach conservation outreach topics. Although mainly limited to articles published in either English or other European languages, a search on the term "outreach" in Getty AATA Online, a database of articles that have been published by heritage conservators and scientists, gives a sense of the state of outreach in the conservation field (GCI n.d.). The results show a distinct increase in articles published on outreach starting in the early 2000s, with the majority in this area noted from the mid-2010s onward. Similarly, the term "engagement" has grown in the number of articles starting around the same time. A 2013 position paper outlining the goals of the AIC K-12 Working Group defines the advantages of K-12 outreach activities and provides concrete strategies for conservators to engage with both classroom educators and students (AIC K-12 Working Group 2013). *Playing to the Galleries and Engaging New Audiences: The Public Face of Conservation*, a volume based on talks presented at a 2011 conference in Williamsburg, VA, was published in 2013 and is still one of the main publications devoted specifically to the topic of cultural heritage conservation outreach. Included in the

2011 conference and the book are two articles discussing K-12 (aged five to eighteen) outreach from the perspective of conservators. The first article, by conservators Sarah Barack and Beth Edelstein, explores the value of collaborations between classroom educators and conservators to ensure programming fits required standards (Barack and Edelstein 2013). The second article is Colleen Snyder's *Behind the Scenes at the Getty Villa: Conservation Outreach for Kids* that presents hands-on activities during a public event at the Getty Villa (Snyder 2013). These examples showcase the importance of having multiple skilled facilitators to create effectively tailored lessons for young children. Although a number of publications devoted to outreach and engagement have followed, these tend to be single articles or have a broader focus on community engagement, such as *Heritage Conservation and Social Engagement* (Peters et al. 2020).

In most cases, the increased production of resources and cultural heritage outreach has prioritized adults and older students. In a recent survey conducted by the Education Outreach (K-12) Subcommittee of the American Institute for Conservation, more than 65% of respondents had done some sort of outreach to audiences aged three to eighteen, with almost 90% doing outreach with school groups. Of the respondents, only 17% had done any programming for early learners; however, there are fewer resources focusing on this area (AIC 2022). One of the contributing factors to this phenomenon is that conservators are often in a position where they are developing their own outreach materials. As such, the familiarity and knowledge of communicating with adults and college to high school aged students often shapes the types of programs offered.

A noteworthy trend from this survey suggests that when conservators can collaborate with youth and family educators, there is greater comfort with creating public programming and resources about conservation. Supported by case studies presented throughout this book, it becomes evident that conservation topics can be designed successfully for early learners. While conservators have expertise in the subject matter, educators know how to present the material to these younger audiences. In addition to their experience working with early learners, different types of educators (such as teachers, instructors, program organizers, and facilitators) bring expertise in specific learning contexts, including schools, museums, and after school programs. The collaboration of conservators with a range of educators can provide an opportunity for preservation outreach to be tailored to various types of programming.

In this way, the public engagement and academic publication reflect a growing consensus that the preservation of cultural heritage should not be limited solely to aspiring professionals or individuals in academic and school-based settings. As conservation continues to become more visible to the public, programming can be expanded to more diverse audiences, including early learners and families (Chase et al. 2023).

Opening Doors: Tailoring Conservation Outreach for Early Learners

As cultural heritage preservation engages with younger audiences, programming and resources need to be customized to meet their needs. Early childhood encompasses those who are in the initial stages of formal learning, which ranges from birth to around eight years old, depending on the educational system and regional guidelines (NAEYC (National Association for the Education of Young Children) Governing Board 2020, U.S. Department of Education 2022). In this book, case studies primarily concentrate on cultural heritage programming for early learners aged three to eight. Notably, conservation-based outreach involving children under the age of three was not readily available, which indicates a potential area for future exploration and research. In the seven examples included in this volume, young children encounter cultural heritage preservation in formal and informal learning environments, both of which provide meaningful avenues for exploring the subject matter. Formal learning environments can provide more structured and curriculum-aligned instruction, like the "Art Matters" after-school club detailed in Chapter 9 that features grade-appropriate enrichment activities tailored to the International Baccalaureate (IB) curriculum. Other case studies highlight how informal learning environments, such as museums, foster open-ended exploration and interactivity. In Chapter 6, the Heritage Conservation Centre supports an informal learning environment for young children in its Little Conservators program, where participants learn about preventive conservation through songs and storytelling. Sharing cultural heritage preservation with early learners can take many forms, providing conservators and scientists with a range of possibilities depending on resources and available collaborators.

During early childhood, children undergo significant developmental milestones, including physical, cognitive, social, and emotional growth (American Academy of Pediatrics n.d.). To meet the developmental needs of early learners, there are certain elements that are necessary to ensure age-appropriate learning (Young et al. 2022). In this book, case studies explore how to introduce artworks and cultural heritage practices in an age-appropriate manner. For example, in Chapter 8, the Cleveland Museum of Art highlights the importance of engaging young children with works of art, which gives children an opportunity to interact with objects that they would not encounter otherwise, and shares how to use appropriate language to relate unfamiliar artifacts with the life experiences of young learners, affirming research that demonstrates that young children can retain enduring and vivid memories from museum visits, which includes artifacts and ideas that were introduced (Falk and Dierking 2016). Other examples in this book demonstrate how storytelling can be used to provide essential context for the activities being presented to early learners, like Jenny Mathiasson's "Low Cost, High Fun" case study in Chapter 5. With the appropriate adjustments made, cultural heritage programming can be tailored to early learners and provide meaningful engagement opportunities.

Present throughout all the case studies is evidence that young children learn through interactive play and exploration that engages multiple senses and prior knowledge (Cope and Kalantzis 2000). In this book, all programs incorporate aspects of guided play, which is a pedagogical approach where adults provide early learners space to explore and make choices on their own terms (Hirsh-Pasek et al. 2008). Affirming the value of this teaching method, recent studies indicate that guided play provides early learners with stronger learning outcomes in numeracy and behavior skills than free play or direct instruction (Skene et al. 2022). Inherent in play-based learning is the fact that children learn and process memories through movement.[3] As educators and conservators adapt cultural heritage preservation programming for early learners, incorporating movement and interactivity into lesson plans, such as moving through exhibitions or conserving their own artworks, are essential for this audience's engagement with and retention of the material.

On a societal level, there is profound value in expanding cultural heritage preservation outreach to early learners. Studies suggest high-quality early childhood programs can have several long-term benefits: promoting education, reducing crime, raising earnings, and even improving health (Campbell et al. 2014). In addition to these positive outcomes, the National Association for the Education of Young Children provides guidance on how to approach early childhood education through an equity lens, which contributes to broader societal goals of fostering equal access to education and reducing disparities in society (Moses 2023). By integrating equity-focused approaches into cultural heritage programs, conservators and educators will not only nurture the potential of upcoming generations but also take concrete steps towards building a more inclusive future.

Nurturing STEAM Curiosity: Cultivating Conservation Outreach for Young Minds

STEM education, a term initiated by the National Science Foundation, is a pedagogical approach that focuses on one or more of the four disciplines of Science, Technology, Engineering, and Mathematics (National Science Foundation 2013). Researchers revealed that informal learning environments, such as field trips, "aided first grade students in developing more sophisticated science content knowledge when the field trip was combined with formal instruction" (Alexandre et al. 2022). This suggests that informal learning environments can stimulate STEM interest and develop social-emotional skills. As research demonstrates, these informal educational environments (including museums) can provide a uniquely positive environment to foster learning by young children (Munley 2012). Early learning experiences have the potential to enhance children's readiness to engage in science learning in school and encourage lifelong STEM pursuits (Hurst et al. 2019).

Building on STEM, STEAM-based education integrates Art and Design in conjunction with Science, Technology, Engineering, and Mathematics. Georgette Yakman, credited with being the founding researcher in STEAM educational framework in 2006, explains that "STEAM is about more than converging the fine arts and design thinking into STEAM fields. The liberal arts are, the 'who & why,' the reasoning, to the 'what & how' of STEM" (Yakman 2019). The Rhode Island School of Design, an early champion of STEAM education, actively fosters "cross-disciplinary exploration into various studio practices" throughout its curriculum and academic offerings (Rhode Island School of Design n.d.). Over the past fifteen years, STEAM education has gained widespread recognition and adoption.

This form of arts integration connects the arts through science. The Kennedy Center defines arts integration as "an approach to teaching in which students construct and demonstrate understanding through an art form. Students engage in a creative process which connects an art form and another subject and meets evolving objectives." (Kennedy Center, n.d.). Research has shown that arts integration improves long-term retention of content and skills related to executive function such as inhibitory control, working memory, and flexible thinking. Additionally, arts integration strategies have been linked to improved student engagement and social-emotional skills (Carey 2017). Since STEAM-based arts integration serves as an access point for guided inquiry, dialogue, and critical thinking (Riley 2020), the Smithsonian Institution has created STEAM-focused lessons across its 21 museums and the National Zoo throughout the past decade. The annual Smithsonian National Education Summit hosts a national group of K-12 educators to discuss current trends and policies, as well as featuring relevant Smithsonian instructional resources. The main theme of the 2023 summit was "Together We Thrive: Fostering a Sense of Belonging" with two of the four tracks of the summit highlighting STEAM education and arts integration (Smithsonian Institution 2023).

At its core, conservation outreach is inherently a STEAM-based endeavor, since it combines art, science, and history. There are many choices in offering STEAM-based conservation programming in museums, such as a one-time program or repeated series, youth or intergenerational family offerings, and school partnership or public programs. This book delves into practical STEAM models, offering examples that highlight their real-word application. These span from school partnerships, like the Michael C. Carlos Museum's collaboration with Briarlake Elementary School in Atlanta in Chapter 10, to innovative programs within a museum setting, such as the American University of Beirut Archaeological Museum's Children's Program in Chapter 7.

While preserving cultural material is essential, the field of cultural heritage conservation must also prioritize the cultivation of sustained support across diverse audience segments to ensure continuity. For the profession to maintain cultural relevance and community support, there needs to be an acknowledgement and awareness of the importance of cultural heritage and its preservation. Just as exposure to other topics at an early age has been found to be invaluable to long-term development of knowledge, so too is this the case for cultural heritage conservation. Cross-disciplinary educational research presented in this chapter demonstrates the value and impact it can have on future generations when we appreciate, invest in, and sustain cultural heritage.

Notes

1 Rutherford J. Gettens arrived at the Freer Gallery of Art (now part of the National Museum of Asian Art) from Harvard University's Fogg Art Museum in 1951 and brought with him a scientific approach to the conservation and research of artworks. For a more in-depth examination of the development of conservation, see Francesca Bewer's *A Laboratory for Art* (Bewer 2010).
2 There are a variety of national and international standards or code of ethics for the profession, but most have similar fundamentals. The Icon and AIC code of ethics are just two examples (ICON 2020, AIC 1994).
3 For more on how movement can be incorporated for early learners in a museum setting, see "Part II: Museum Spaces" in Hackett, Holmes, and MacRae (2020, 75–131). Total Physical Response (TPR) is one example of how K-12 educators are incorporating movement into language learning and vocabulary lesson plans. See Erin Walton, "An introduction to Total Physical Response (and four activities to try)," Education First, Accessed 3 October, 2023: https://teacherblog.ef.com/total-physical-response-efl-classroom/.

References

Alexandre, Suzanne, Yaoying Xu, Melissa Washington-Nortey, and Chinchih Chen. 2022. "Informal STEM learning for young children: A Systematic Literature Review." *International Journal of Environmental Research and Public Health, 19* (14): 8299. Accessed 6 November, 2022. https://doi.org/10.3390/ijerph19148299.

AIC (American Institute for Conservation). n.d. "What is Conservation?" Accessed 14 July, 2023. https://www.culturalheritage.org/about-conservation/what-is-conservation.

———. 1994. "Our Code of Ethics." Revised August 1994. Accessed 25 September, 2023. https://www.culturalheritage.org/about-conservation/code-of-ethics.

———. 2013. "AIC Position Paper: Beyond Career Day: Conservation and K-12 Education." May 24, 2013. https://www.culturalheritage.org/docs/default-source/resources/administration/governance/position-papers-and-statements/position-paper-on-conservation-and-k-12-education-(may-2013).pdf?sfvrsn=d9393b1d_16.

———. 2022. "Conservation K-12 Outreach Programs Survey." January 12, 2022. https://www.culturalheritage.org/docs/default-source/publications/reports/survey-reports/conservation-k-12-outreach-programs-survey-report.pdf?sfvrsn=3eca1520_4.

———. 2023. "Ask a Conservator Day." Accessed 7 November, 2023. https://www.culturalheritage.org/about-conservation/what-is-conservation/conservation-in-social-media/ask-a-conservator-day.

———. 2023. "K-12 Educational Resources on Conservation." AIC Wiki. Last modified on October 17, 2023. https://www.conservation-wiki.com/wiki/K12_Educational_Resources_on_Conservation.

American Academy of Pediatrics. n.d. "2 Month – 5 Relational Health Developmental Milestones Timeline." Accessed 23 September, 2023. https://www.aap.org/en/patient-care/early-childhood/milestone-timeline/.

Ashmolean, Museum. n.d. "The Conservation Galleries." Accessed 5 November, 2023. https://www.ashmolean.org/conservation-galleries.

Barack, Sarah, and Beth Edelstein. 2013. "From One Student to Many: Multi-Level Approaches to Conservation Outreach in the K-12 Arena." In *The Public Face of Conservation*, edited by Emily Williams, 96–103. London: Archetype Publications Ltd.

Bewer, Francesca. 2010. *A Laboratory for Art: Harvard's Fogg Museum and the Emergence of Conservation in America, 1900-1950*. Cambridge, MA: Harvard University Art Museums. distributed by Yale University Press.

Campbell, Frances, Gabriella Conti, James J. Heckman, Seong Hyeok Moon, Rodrigo Pinto, Elizabeth Pungello, and Yi Pan. 2014. "Early Childhood Investments Substantially Boost Adult Health." *Science* 343, issue 6178 (March 28): 1478–1485. https://www.science.org/doi/10.1126/science.1248429.

Carey, and Lisa. 2017. *What Is Arts Integration?* Kennedy Krieger Institute. December 5, 2–17. https://www.kennedykrieger.org/stories/linking-research-classrooms-blog/what-arts-integration.

Chase, Ellen, Leah Bright, Laura Hoffman, and Matthew Lasnoski. 2023. "Planting the seeds of conservation: Sustaining the past by investing in our future." In *Working Towards a Sustainable Past. ICOM-CC 20th Triennial Conference, Valencia, 18-22 September 2023*, edited by J. Bridgeland. Paris: International Council of Museums.

Cope, Bill, and Mary Kalantzis. eds. 2000. *Multiliteracies: Literacy Learning and Design of Social Futures*. London: Routledge.

Falk, John, and Lynn Dierking. 2016. *The Museum Experience Revisited*. New York: Routledge.

Getty Conservation Institute. n.d. "Outreach." Getty AATA Online. Accessed 15 June, 2023. https://aata.getty.edu/primo-explore/search?query=any,contains,outreach&tab=aata&search_scope=AATA&vid=AATA&offset=0.

Hackett, Abigail, Rachel Holmes, and Christina MacRae. 2020. *Working with Young Children in Museums: Weaving Theory and Practice*. New York: Routledge.

Hirsh-Pasek, Kathy, Roberta Golinkoff, Laura Berk, and Dorothy Singer. 2008. *A Mandate for Playful Learning in School: Presenting the Evidence*. Oxford: Oxford University Press.

Horwitz, Jeff. 2019. "Why Life Hack Videos Seem Too Good to be True. (They Are)." *Wall Street Journal*. October 10, 2019. Accessed 14 September, 2022. https://www.wsj.com/articles/long-story-short-my-microwave-exploded-the-problem-with-life-hack-videos-11570636955.

Hurst, Michelle, Naomi Polinsky, Catherine Haden, Susan Levine, and David Uttal. 2019. "Leveraging Research on Informal Learning to Inform Policy on Promoting Early STEM." *Social Policy Report*, 32 (3): 1–33. https://doi.org/10.1002/sop2.5.

ICOM-CC (International Council of Museums – Committee for Conservation). n.d. "Terminology for Conservation." Accessed 14 July, 2023. https://www.icom-cc.org/en/terminology-for-conservation.

ICON (The Institute of Conservation). 2020. "The Icon Ethical Guidance." June 20, 2020. https://www.icon.org.uk/resource/icon-ethical-guidance.html.

Kennedy Center. "What is Arts Integration?" n.d. Accessed 6 November, 2022. https://www.kennedy-center.org/education/resources-for-educators/classroom-resources/articles-and-how-tos/articles/collections/arts-integration-resources/what-is-arts-integration/.

McClure, Ian. 2013. "Making Exhibitions of Ourselves." In *The Public Face of Conservation*, edited by Emily Williams, 163–169. London: Archetype Publications Ltd.

Meloni, Sabrina, and Quentin Buvelot. 2023. *Facelifts & Makeovers*: Educating a Larger Audience about the Mysteries and Challenges of Conservation. In *Working Towards a Sustainable Past. ICOM-CC 20th Triennial Conference Preprints, Valencia, 18–22 September 2023*, ed. J. Bridgland. Paris: International Council of Museums.

Metropolitan Museum of Art. n.d. "MetKids Microscope." Accessed 4 November, 2023. https://www.metmuseum.org/perspectives/series/metkids-microscope.

Moses, Annie. 2023. "Advances in Understanding Child Development and Learning Through a Lens of Equity," *Young Learners* 78, no. 3 (September 2023). https://www.naeyc.org/resources/pubs/yc/fall2023/child-development-through-equity-lens.

Munley, Mary. 2012. *Early Learning in Museums: A Review of Literature*. Smithsonian Institution's Early Learning Collaborative Network and Smithsonian Early Enrichment Center. Washington, DC: Smithsonian Institution. https://www.si.edu/Content/SEEC/docs/mem%20literature%20review%20early%20learning%20in%20museums%20final%204%2012%202012.pdf.

Museum of Fine Arts Boston. 2021. "Conservation in Action: Japanese Buddhist Sculptures." August 1, 2021. https://www.mfa.org/collections/conservation/conservation-in-action/japanese-buddhist-sculptures.

NAEYC (National Association for the Education of Young Children) Governing Board. April 2020. "Developmentally Appropriate Practice." National Association for Education of Young Children. https://www.naeyc.org/sites/default/files/globally shared/downloads/PDFs/resources/position-statements/dap-statement_0.pdf.

NMAH (National Museum of American History, Smithsonian Institution). *Star Spangled Banner: The Preservation Project*. Accessed 9 October, 2023. https://amhistory.si.edu/starspangledbanner/preservation-project.aspx.

National Science Foundation. 2013. "Inspiring STEM Learning." Accessed 6 November, 2022. https://www.nsf.gov/about/congress/reports/ehr_research.pdf.

Peters, Renata, Iris den Boer, Jessica Johnson, and Susanna Pancaldo, eds. 2020. *Heritage Conservation and Social Engagement*. London: UCL Press. https://discovery.ucl.ac.uk/id/eprint/10115572/1/Heritage-Conservation-and-Social-Engagement.pdf.

Rijksmuseum. 2023. "Mission Masterpiece." Accessed 27 September, 2023. https://www.rijksmuseum.nl/en/whats-on/exhibitions/past/mission-masterpiece.

Riley, Susan. 2020. *What Is STEAM Education? A Comprehensive Guide for K-12 Schools*. The Institute for Arts Integration and STEAM. Accessed 6 November, 2022. https://artsintegration.com/what-is-steam-education-in-k-12-schools/.

Rhode Island School of Design. n.d. "STEAM." Accessed 13 November 13. https://www.risd.edu/steam

Skene, Kayleigh, Christine O'Farrelly, Elizabeth Byrne, Natalie Kirby, Eloise Stevens, and Paul Ramchandani. 2022. "Can Guidance During Play Enhance Children's

Learning and Development in Educational Contexts? A Systematic Review and Meta-Analysis." *Child Development*, 93(4) (July/August): 1162–1180. https://srcd. onlinelibrary.wiley.com/doi/10.1111/cdev.13730#cdev13730-bib-0023.

Smithsonian American Art Museum. n.d. "Lunder Conservation Center." Accessed 7 November, 2023. https://americanart.si.edu/art/conservation.

Smithsonian Institution. "National Education Summit 2023." Accessed November 1, 2023. https://www.si.edu/educators/national-education-summit-2023.

Snyder, Colleen. 2013. "Behind the Scenes at the Getty Villa: Conservation Outreach for Kids." In *The Public Face of Conservation*, edited by Emily Williams, 113–120. London: Archetype Publications Ltd.

U.S. Department of Education. 2022. "Early Learning: About early learning." 2022. Accessed November 6, 2023. https://www2.ed.gov/about/inits/ed/earlylearning/about. html.

Walton, Erin. "An introduction to Total Physical Response (and four activities to try)." Education First. Accessed October 3, 2023. https://teacherblog.ef.com/ total-physical-response-efl-classroom/.

Yakman, Georgette. "STEAM - An Educational Framework to Relate Things to Each Other and Reality." K12 Digest. December 2019. https://www.k12digest.com/steam-an-educational-framework-to-relate-things-to-each-other-and-reality/. Quoted in Joseph Lathan. "Why STEAM is so Important to 21st Century Education." University of San Diego. Accessed on November 13, 2023. https://onlinedegrees.sandiego.edu/ steam-education-in-schools/.

Young, Sarah, Tricia Eadier, Liz Suda, and Amelia Church. 2022. "LEARN: Essential Elements of Museum Education Programs for Young Children." *Curator: The Museum Journal* 65 (1(January): 209–223.

Part I

Smithsonian Institution's Art & Me Program

The first portion of this book focuses on an in-depth exploration of a multi-year cultural heritage conservation program tailored for early learners and their caregivers. The Smithsonian Institution's "Art & Me" program is an illuminating conservation outreach workshop hosted at the National Museum of Asian Art and Smithsonian American Art Museum in Washington, DC, since 2016.

In Chapter 2, we delve into the origins and evolution of the Art & Me program, looking at its development, the expansion of the program across the Smithsonian, and overcoming barriers. Chapter 3 provides detailed information on the format of the Art & Me program for both in-person and virtual environments. We discuss the program's structure, breaking down components and detailed examples that make up the workshops. In the final chapter of this section, we provide an overview of the feedback, a review of the evaluation of the Art & Me program, and guidance on how to build institutional evaluative capacity for using informal and formal methods. Recognizing the need to substantiate the value of our programs, we describe tools and methodologies used to assess and measure participant experiences.

Throughout Part I, we offer a comprehensive understanding of Art & Me's development, structure, and evaluation processes to highlight how this type of outreach can foster cross-disciplinary approaches to reaching early learners. To this end, we hope to inspire additional cultural heritage conservation public engagement for this audience.

DOI: 10.4324/9781003333210-2

2 Developing an Intergenerational Arts Integration Program

Ellen Chase, Laura Hoffman, and Matthew Lasnoski

Early Learning Programming at the National Museum of Asian Art

In response to a yearlong review of program offerings in 2015, Youth & Family Programs Manager Matthew Lasnoski embarked on piloting new youth and family programs at the National Museum of Asian Art (NMAA). A survey identified that nearly half of the family programs audiences were under the age of seven, despite the museum's youth program being advertised for children eight and up. The creation of the Art & Me program came about as a fortunate convergence of this demonstrated interest in early learners programming and a recognition that cultural heritage conservation was a relatively unexplored area for this age group.

Objects Conservator Ellen Chase had previous experience leading conservation programs with early learners through collaborations with the Smithsonian Early Enrichment Center. It had become clear to Ellen that when introduced in an appropriate way, engaging with young children about the ideas of cultural heritage preservation was a great opportunity to form an early bond and create an experience for them to build on as they grew. Although very interested in going further, particularly for this age group, she knew it was critical to collaborate with an educator to make the sessions engaging and accessible for early learners, as well as ensure internal support within the conservation department. With the support of Donna Strahan, Head of the Department of Conservation and Scientific Research, Ellen reached out to Matthew to develop a sustained program at the museum to broaden the approach and have access to the museum collections. As a result, a collaboration emerged between the Public Programs and the Conservation and Scientific Research departments at the museum. By combining resources and expertise, Ellen and Matthew were able to establish Art & Me, the first dedicated registration-based workshop series for early learners and their adult companions at the museum.

DOI: 10.4324/9781003333210-3

Getting Started

Despite the demand for programs targeting early learners, there were limited staff and budgetary resources available for piloting the Art & Me program, particularly because there was some initial skepticism regarding the effectiveness of cultural heritage conservation workshops for early learners. Although we had previous experience working with this audience, we had never developed a cohesive, ongoing program series related to cultural heritage preservation for early learners. Knowing the great potential for outreach to this age group, we decided that it would be necessary to demonstrate the efficacy of these efforts to establish institutional support. As a first step, a pilot program was established to experiment with a variety of methods to determine what approach would work best in the museum.

We considered various possibilities, including a program for school groups. However, we decided to develop the initial test as a family program to leverage intergenerational collaboration to facilitate learning about cultural heritage preservation. Recent research has found that family visits are a determining factor in whether someone will continue to visit museums in adulthood, and this was taken into account in terms of our planning.[1] By creating a family program structure, both early learners and their adult companions would be exposed to the ideas of cultural heritage conservation, no matter their age. Additionally, a family program structure allowed more individualized attention for the early learner participants since they work together with their caregivers during the sessions.

For the initial pilot program in May 2016, we looked for themes and ideas in the collection and special exhibitions that could be discussed in the first workshop. Since the program did not have its own dedicated funding source, we proposed that this first Art & Me program be included in the programming related to the museum's special exhibition, *Peacock Room REMIX: Darren Waterston's "Filthy Lucre."* At NMAA, special exhibitions receive dedicated funding for outreach and education, so it is more conducive to new programming ideas. Through the process of selecting a first workshop topic, we were cognizant of our institution's funding structure to help get the program off the ground with a long-term goal to focus more on the museum's permanent collection. We hoped this pilot program would help serve as evidence that the program was successful to seek dedicated funding for the program later.

The exhibition featured a reimagined version of James McNeill Whistler's Peacock Room as "a decadent ruin collapsing on itself" (NMAA (National Museum of Asian Art) n.d.). The installation featured broken ceramics and shelving, which leant itself to a discussion of the field of conservation in general, as well as physical damage and careful handling. When developing the pilot Art & Me program, the objective was to limit the concepts introduced to a manageable size appropriate for early learners. Even from this early stage, the decision was made to utilize the ten main threats to cultural heritage items, known as the Ten Agents of Deterioration, as a basis for the program focus (CCI (Canadian Conservation Institute) n.d.). Commonly used in cultural heritage conservation outreach for older age groups, the focus on one agent of deterioration per session seemed a good place to start building a program specifically for families with early learners.

The modest budget for the first program went towards buying child-size lab coats and making buttons for the youth participants (Figure 2.1). The reason we invested in these materials was to invite program participants to join the program as conservators-in-training. Our intention was to foster an element of guided play and actively involve the children in the discovery of what a conservator is and does in a museum since research has shown that this approach helps young learners engage and learn.[2] Although the program staff needed to purchase some new materials, the public programs and conservation teams drew on their existing supplies and resources. Gloves for the conservators-in-training were supplied from existing inventory, and Ellen brought equipment from the lab for hand-on demonstrations, such as dusting brushes and plastic droppers. Material lists for art making were taken from supplies already in stock in the museum's studio. Having a collaborative partnership, we were able to prioritize and brainstorm through creating an activity list together.

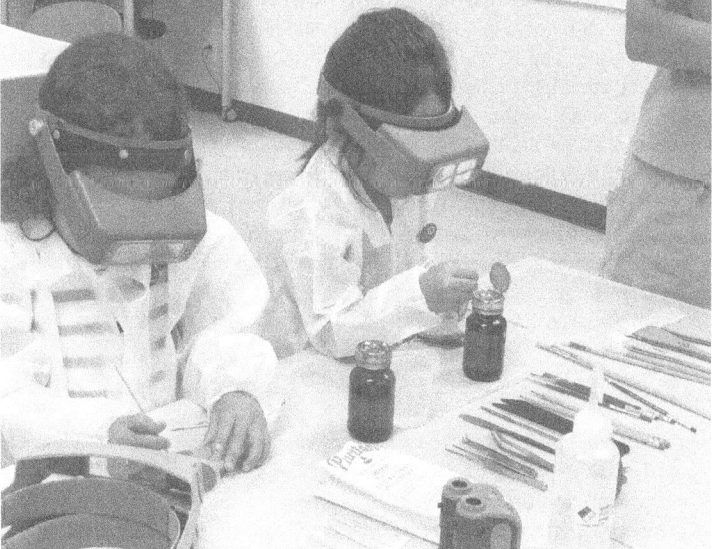

Figure 2.1 Art & Me participants dressed as "art doctors" and exploring conservation tools.

Image courtesy of National Museum of Asian Art, Smithsonian Institution; photo by Laura Hoffman.

Another advantage of selecting a special exhibition for our first workshop was the additional marketing potential for the new program. Since we did not have a dedicated audience, we needed additional promotion and outreach to reach our intended audience. *Peacock Room REMIX* was our newest exhibition with a sizable promotion budget and other programs. Since we aligned the Art & Me pilot program to this large museum priority, the program benefitted from additional promotion and each session filled up with a waiting list.

Compared to other established family programs, the lesson plan for the first Art & Me program took longer since there was no existing template. The planning for the first program took nearly five months from the initial approval to implementation. We met every other week to develop and try out different aspects. The meeting time was spent thinking through new elements, establishing roles and responsibilities, and testing out ideas. Additionally, we were supported by interns who helped prep and test out materials for the hands-on activity.

From the first program, it was critical for us to learn from the audience about their experience and demonstrate to museum leadership the value of the program. From the outset, we used informal and formal means to gather audience feedback. The first method was to collect qualitative feedback from program participants by putting up large sheets of paper on the walls next to post-it notes with prompts to elicit feedback on their experience. This informal method was able to capture unfiltered feedback and allowed early learners a chance to participate in a fun way that could help structure future iterations of the program. The second method for audience feedback was through a paper survey completed immediately after the program. Only caregivers could provide feedback on these surveys since there is a strict age limit for surveying visitors at the Smithsonian Institution. The surveys were used to collect feedback on the audience's experiences and demographic information. The results from these surveys and open-ended responses were analyzed to identify successes and pain points in the visitor experience, which will be illustrated further in Chapter 4, as well as to look at demographic information that could be used for targeting future outreach and assessing which marketing efforts provided the largest return on investment.

Becoming an Ongoing Series

Since the initial program received positive visitor feedback and was at capacity, we had a compelling case to continue the program. From 2017 to 2019, the Art & Me program was offered two-to-three times during the school year as an onsite program for children and their caregivers on weekends. During this phase, we focused on developing lesson plans that highlighted the museum's collections and the Ten Agents of Deterioration. This transition away from special exhibitions allowed additional connection to artworks that Ellen and other conservators had treated at the museum and allowed for more detailed, compelling stories to be told about the artworks.

In the 2017 budget year, the Public Programs department was able to allocate a modest budget to buy new resources for programs, providing new avenues of engagement and interactive activities. In our second workshop, we focused on introducing the concept of what a conservator is and does in a museum. With the additional budget, we purchased supplies for more specialized program activities, including post-program enrichment. Participants made their own conservation tool kits during this workshop to continue their observations at home with objects that were precious and belonged to them.

Furthermore, a dedicated budget for the program allowed us to be less dependent on the specific artworks and themes contained in temporary exhibitions. The dedicated budget allowed us to spend between 100 and 200 USD per workshop on materials. As a result, we were able to develop a more consistent approach to presenting the museum's collections. For instance, a workshop entitled, "Silver Tells a Story," featured silver vessels from the museum's Ancient Near Eastern collection and looked at the effect of airborne pollutants. In preparation for the workshop, we purchased tarnished silver objects on eBay to allow participants a hands-on experience working with these materials and procured sterling silver disk pendants for the take-home component.

From 2017 to 2019, audience development was key to the long-term success of Art & Me. Our initial goal was to meet the demonstrated need to create more age-appropriate programs for early learners, which meant that we started by inviting existing audiences with young children to try a new program offering. We handed out printed flyers at other family programs and encouraged families to register. We also included the programs in the museum's monthly e-newsletter and created Facebook events to help attract those already familiar with the museum. For our existing family audiences, it was appreciated that we diversified our program offerings and provided such a unique art workshop that incorporated science. In addition to encouraging adoption of the new program by our existing audience, we sought to attract new audiences. We worked on developing key relationships with individuals and organizations that could help us broaden the reach of the program ranging from the Smithsonian Early Enrichment Center to Washington, DC, family bloggers.

Expansion of the Art & Me Program across the Smithsonian Institution

In 2018, Laura Hoffman joined as Program Manager at the Smithsonian American Art Museum's (SAAM) Lunder Conservation Center. Since the Lunder Conservation Center is a visible lab, this position is integral for the center's objective to engage audiences in art conservation (Figure 2.2). In hiring Laura, SAAM's Head of Conservation Amber Kerr made a deliberate shift to increase educational outreach and to target new audiences. In Laura's

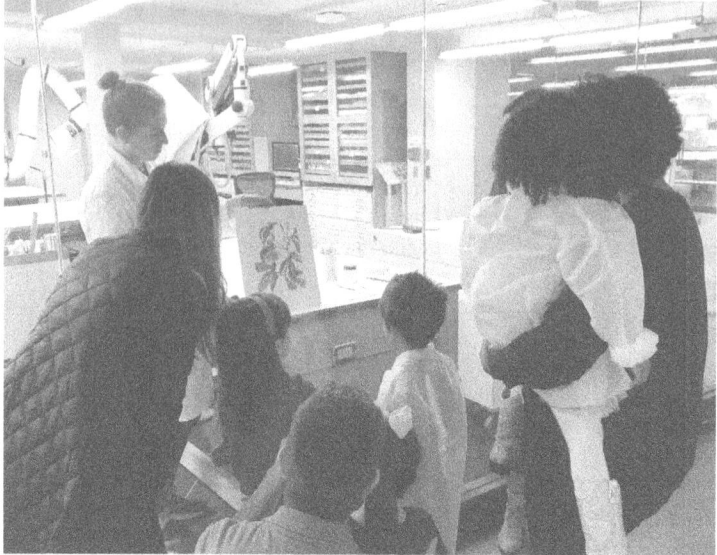

Figure 2.2 SAAM's Lunder Conservation Center staff interacting with Art & Me participants through the visible conservation lab windows.

Image courtesy of Smithsonian American Art Museum; photo by Ellen Chase.

previous positions as a museum educator, she had experience with early learning and family programming and saw great potential to broaden the audience base to a younger demographic while targeting intergenerational audiences.

Laura came into the position with knowledge of NMAA's Art and Me program through her previous volunteer work for family festivals with Matthew. During her first year at Lunder, she connected with Matthew and Ellen to observe and assist with the Art & Me program to better understand the program and to gauge their interest in offering Art & Me as a pan-institutional series across both museums. In 2019, the three of us teamed up to officially launch the Smithsonian partnership, increasing the series from biannually to quarterly programming split across NMAA and SAAM.

In joining forces, the program bolstered its offerings, not only in terms of the number of workshops but also in terms of the types of artworks considered in the programming and the workshop format. The workshops were planned in collaboration with the two institutions, resulting in a year-long schedule of programs designed to complement and build on each other. During this phase of the expansion, we explored various models of early learning education. After attending the Smithsonian Early Learning Collaborative's "One Good Thing: Museums and Early Learning" professional development workshop in May 2019, we refined our methodology to incorporate other Smithsonian Institution early learning models. One of the changes included structuring the warm-ups around the central activity to introduce the overall theme. Another shift was moving away from one activity to a variety for participants to pick and choose. The activities focused more on interaction, fun, and play. By making the program less instructional, Art & Me evolved into a more interactive program based on guided learning, which worked better for the early learning demographic.

Furthermore, as part of this refinement, the team began seeking additional partnerships to increase the number of first-time participants for Art & Me. We made efforts to increase outreach to audiences who may not typically be aware of the early learning programs at the Smithsonian. For example, we participated in a Smithsonian-wide initiative that provided transportation to various museums for local DC families who had not previously visited the Smithsonian Institution. During one of these sessions, children and caregivers came to NMAA to learn about light damage in relation to the making and care of prints. The focus in this session was not only to introduce the concept of cultural heritage preservation and its importance to early learners and their caregivers, but also to introduce the museum as a fun and welcoming place.

Going Online

When the global COVID-19 pandemic hit in March 2020, all in-person programs were put on hiatus with no sense of when they would return. Like many all over the world, we had to regroup and adapt. Over the spring, Laura had begun introducing conservation-related online programs for adults at the Lunder Conservation Center, and by the summer, we launched the first online family Art & Me programs (Figure 2.3).

Art & Me became one of the first early learning programs to transition to virtual at the Smithsonian, so there were few models to refer to. Rather than trying to offer exactly the same program as the in-person experience, the team experimented with the format to determine what worked best online. We wanted to maintain the main objectives of the original program: introduce art conservation and preservation, showcase the importance through real-world examples, and practice hands-on skills through art making. As with the in-person programs, the virtual Art & Me would be geared for early learners and their caregivers. The first online program took place via Zoom webinar in July 2020 with outdoor sculpture as the focus.

Since the pandemic, the team has run numerous online programs, adjusting the time length, flow, and structure based on participant feedback. While consistently offering the program to be forty-five minutes on Saturday mornings, originally the program included a full forty-five minutes of instructional time, which proved to be too long for the age group online and did not provide enough participant-facilitator interaction. As a result, we shortened the instructional portion to thirty minutes before a virtual participant show-and-tell to foster a more interactive program.

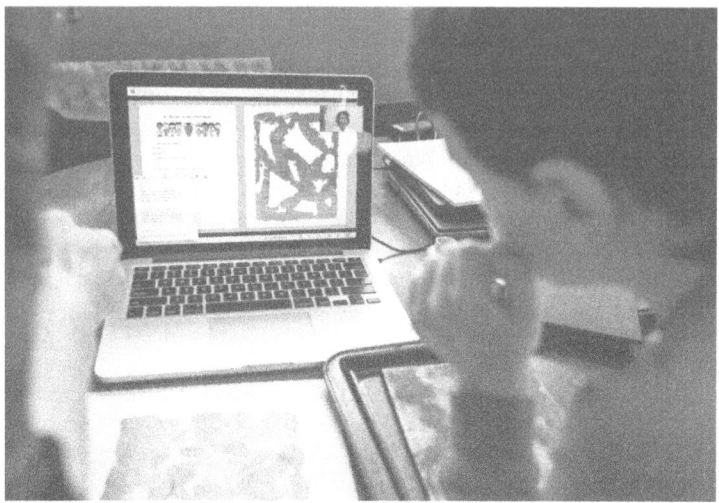

Figure 2.3 Art & Me online workshop about prints and light damage.
Photo by Brian S. Allard.

Pre-pandemic, we provided art supplies for the in-person Art & Me programs. When switching to the online format, we wanted to ensure the art activity would continue to be approachable. For each program, our art activities use common, budget-friendly art supplies that families likely have at home already. As an added measure, we provide ideas for substitutions, so all attendees are able to participate.

While online programming has its challenges, it has also been highly rewarding. Virtual programming has provided a platform for truly collaborative work. Before, the pan-institutional Art & Me workshops were plotted out throughout the year together but ran individually at either NMAA or SAAM. When switching to the digital format, we planned collaborative lessons, utilizing conservation stories from both collections and building off of each other for richer lesson scaffolding. During this time of experimentation, we honed our joint effort and established a sense of consistency by having an educator and conservator from each institution to co-facilitate. In addition to the three of us, SAAM Objects Conservator Leah Bright joined the Art & Me team. The addition of Leah's consistent participation has added depth and continuity to the workshops, both in terms of planning and presentation.

Transitioning to digital programming has further expanded the Art & Me reach. Some of the Art & Me online programs have tapped into significantly larger audiences by being part of festivals, such as Lunar New Year and cherry blossom celebrations, garnering hundreds of participants each session. When it comes to workshops inspired by cultural celebrations, we work to integrate community knowledge and expertise into the workshop curriculum. For example, museum staff volunteered to enrich these workshops by sharing their own stories of celebrating Lunar New Year. Additionally, we provide online materials and links to cultural resources to provide greater context for the celebrations. Connecting to these larger cultural celebrations has been a great opportunity to introduce our program to new groups that are looking for social activities that tie into lessons into these cultural events. Overall, the digital platform has allowed the program to reach a wider audience, nationally and internationally, which has been very rewarding.

Chapter Takeaways

In this chapter, the evolution of the Art & Me program was explored, and we hope that readers gain valuable lessons and insights in how to build and sustain similar programs. Three key takeaways emerge: the importance of building relationships, embracing flexibility and evolution, and working within limited resources. Additionally, we emphasize the significance of evaluation in ensuring program effectiveness and continuous improvement, which will be discussed further in Chapter 4.

First and foremost, building relationships is paramount for the success and sustainability of any outreach program. By fostering connections with stakeholders such as parents, educators, community organizations, and volunteers, the program team can cultivate a supportive network. Relationships built on trust and mutual respect facilitate collaboration, open doors to new opportunities, and generate valuable feedback. By actively engaging with the community, professionals can better understand the needs and preferences of the target audience, ultimately improving the program's relevance and impact.

The second takeaway centers around flexibility and evolution. A successful outreach program must adapt to changing circumstances and embrace innovation. Unexpected setbacks, like the temporary closure due to the COVID-19 pandemic, can serve as catalysts for new and creative approaches. Professionals should be open to exploring alternative delivery methods, such as virtual workshops or hybrid formats, to ensure continued engagement during challenging times. Embracing flexibility allows programs to remain resilient, relevant, and accessible. The timeline for implementation will be different based on your institution's goals and resources, but whenever you start something new, anticipate it will take time to figure out and iterate what is going to work best for your situation.

An essential element to flexibility and evolution is embracing collaboration on many different levels. The Art & Me program is a collaboration between early learners and their caregivers and is specifically designed so that there is at least one adult for each group attending. As a family program, the participants are intergenerational, sometimes even with grandparents taking part. The caregivers are just as active as early learners, and it presents an opportunity for outreach to both age groups, including providing caregivers with the language to speak with children about conservation. It's also a collaboration between conservators and museum educators, with each bringing their expertise to every phase of the program.

Working with limited budgets and time is a reality faced by many museums and institutions, and for some, the emphasis on revenue-neutral or even revenue-generating programming is a necessity. However, resource constraints should not hinder creativity or impact. Maximizing the available resources requires strategic planning, collaboration, and leveraging community partnerships. Professionals should identify cost-effective materials and tap into the expertise of other staff members. By prioritizing activities with the greatest impact and using innovative approaches, programs can deliver high-quality experiences while managing their resources effectively. Equally, revenue demands may affect what type of programming is feasible for an institution but should not limit the ability to convey the excitement and importance of cultural heritage conservation. Additionally, it is helpful to keep in mind that content created for income-generating avenues, such as summer camps or fee-based workshops, can be re-purposed for less lucrative but equally impactful outreach opportunities.

In conclusion, professionals looking to build a sustained conservation outreach program for young kids will be different depending on your institution and its goals and objectives. However, establishing relationships, embracing flexibility and evolution, and effectively managing limited resources are vital for success. By applying these insights, professionals can create impactful programs that inspire young minds, foster curiosity, and contribute to the future of art and science education.

Notes

1 Cromartie, Kwon and Welch provide a good discussion of the efficacy of family learning in the introduction of their book *Evaluating Early Learning in Museums: Planning for Our Youngest Visitors* (Cromartie, Kwon and Welch 2021, 3–4).
2 See Sharing Cultural Heritage Preservation with Early Learners section in Chapter 1 for more information on the importance of play for engaging young children.

References

CCI (Canadian Conservation Institute). n.d. "Agents of Deterioration." Accessed 1 October, 2023. https://www.canada.ca/en/conservation-institute/services/agents-deterioration.html.

Cromartie, Nicole, Kyong-Ah Kwon, and Meghan Welch. 2021. *Evaluating Early Learning in Museums: Planning for Our Youngest Visitors*. London: Routledge. https://doi.org/10.4324/9780429340413.

NMAA (National Museum of Asian Art). n.d. "Peacock Room REMIX: Darren Waterson's 'Filthy Lucre'." Accessed 29 September, 2023. https://asia.si.edu/whats-on/exhibitions/peacock-room-remix-darren-waterstons-filthy-lucre/.

3 Facilitating Flexible Guided Programs for Early Learners

Ellen Chase, Laura Hoffman, and Matthew Lasnoski

Introduction: Our Approach

The initial development of the Art & Me program included a deliberate approach to integrate scientific concepts into workshops. Despite iterative experimentation and adaptations made while moving the program online, we consistently integrated STEAM (Science, Technology, Engineering, Art, and Mathematics) pedagogy into lesson plans as a core principle. Due to the inherently scientific nature of conservation, the Art & Me program demonstrates how science and art can be integrated meaningfully into the learning outcomes for outreach workshops designed for young children.[1]

Each session highlights the importance of cultural heritage, the importance of preserving that heritage, the conservation process, and the science behind its manufacture and preservation. Although that sounds like a lot to fit into a single session, particularly forty-five minutes online, each of these aspects are discussed in the context of one specific theme, topic, or type of artwork, allowing the presenters to blend all the information together in a cohesive and age-appropriate way.

While this book discusses a variety of approaches for conservation outreach to early learners, the Art & Me program was designed with a multigenerational audience in mind. This format was chosen to allow for the museums to engage with both young children and their caregivers. By engaging with this audience, we can build activities around the pre-existing relationship the caregiver has with early learners during a workshop and use it to help reinforce learning outcomes. The Art & Me programs provide a consistent structure so that families know what to expect, while maintaining flexibility in our approach to accommodate the participants' interests and engagement, as well as the more specific learning needs of family programs with early learners.

Since 2020, the Art & Me program has been offered four-to-five times a year. Although the featured artworks and activities change with each workshop, the overall structure remains the same. This allows for the content to evolve and be updated while also providing consistency for the families and children who attend multiple times a year. The structure of the Art & Me

DOI: 10.4324/9781003333210-4

program is customized to the needs of early learners as opposed to middle and high school-aged children. As we worked more closely with this audience, we learned that the time of day, length of the program, and level of flexibility are important factors to accommodate families with young children. For instance, in-person workshops are scheduled both in the morning and afternoon to allow families to choose which time works best for a museum excursion. In comparison, virtual sessions are run only once in the morning and for a shorter period of time since there is a more limited attention span in a digital format.

Each workshop in the program is built on three basic concepts that are incorporated into the initial planning steps: connection to art in the collections, causes of deterioration, and connection to the lives of the children participating. In addition to the integration of scientific concepts, each of these elements has been a primary consideration for developing the learning outcomes for each workshop since the program's inception. Whether based on a temporary exhibition or the permanent collection, the planning for each workshop begins with a discussion around potential artworks. The materials of construction and associated conservation issues are woven into the Art & Me workshops activities and demonstrations. This was particularly the case for the initial workshops, where reliance on temporary exhibition budgets and programs being held onsite necessitated a focus on specific artworks included in the exhibitions. While the workshops are structured with the same basic components in both the in-person and virtual formats, they are refined to best fit each of these learning environments.

When selecting artworks and themes, we also consider how potential topics can convey concepts related to deterioration. As an example, we developed an in-person workshop that demonstrated how conservators treat artworks that have been damaged physically. We decided to focus on a several ceramics in the National Museum of Asian Art's (NMAA) Islamic art galleries that had been conserved. After looking over the list of objects in the galleries and their conservation history, several had been previously broken and undergone treatment in the NMAA Department of Conservation and Scientific Research. These artworks were featured during the workshop and allowed a concrete illustration of the idea being presented. Virtual workshops allow us to integrate artworks from both the Smithsonian American Art Museum (SAAM) and NMAA collections into the programming with examples from each museum being used during a workshop. When possible, we use the same artworks throughout the various stages of the program to scaffold, strengthening connections.

The program is structured to help children connect to the world they know. In the Art & Me program, we connect to participants' inherent desire to care for their own prized possessions and this approach is integral to how we frame our explanation of why cultural heritage is important. The sentimental connection to one's favorite stuffed animal or other possession is something tangible and understandable for young children. Additionally, we use language relating to familiar experiences, for example, the parallel of conservators taking care of art and doctors taking care of people. The children are very familiar with the idea of a doctor, and this immediately makes conservation more approachable. After one session we heard a little girl say to her parent, "Mommy, I want to be an art doctor!" The children can put themselves in the role of an art doctor; it's familiar but also an opportunity to explore new ideas and use their imagination. At the beginning of each in-person workshop, we provide youth participants with a disposable lab coat, gloves, and an art doctor in-training pin as a way to demonstrate what a conservator is and does in an art museum. This allows participants to immerse themselves closer to the subject matter and directly interact with the concepts on a physical level.[2] Additionally, Ellen wears a lab coat, gloves, and ID badge for the workshops, furthering the connection. In the virtual format, while it is not possible to provide lab coats and gloves to the participants, Ellen still puts on these conservator accessories and talks with the participants about them during the process.

Art & Me In-Person Format

The in-person workshops are for up to twenty-five people and run for approximately ninety minutes. This timeframe allows for opportunities to take breaks and to enjoy snacks between the different sections of the program. Although we plan how long we intend to spend on each section of the program, we also remain flexible to shift based on the responses and needs of the children participating in a specific session.

The in-person workshops are all free; however, they are registration-based rather than drop-in for better planning of resources and limiting the potential for overcrowding during sessions. Additionally, pre-registration provides us with a means to contact attendees with supplemental materials before and after each workshop. To account for potential attrition, we utilize a waitlist and accept walk-ins when space is available.

Starter Activities

Two or three starter activities take place before the formal program begins to allow children to engage as soon as they arrive. These pre-workshop activities or looking exercises are designed to get the participants thinking about the topic of the program. In past sessions, we have put out familiar objects, like pencils or pieces of fabric, for them to examine with magnifying glasses or mini kid-friendly microscopes to get them thinking about close looking. The starter activities relate to artworks or activities that will be introduced later in the program and effectively draw the children in without them realizing it. In one case, participants were so immersed in the experience that we were halfway through a workshop when a child inquired, "When does it start?"

Introduction to Cultural Heritage Conservation

Each workshop always includes several minutes to introduce the concept of cultural heritage conservation. Although there are many repeat families who know what conservation is, it is important to cover it for any new families as well as reinforce the concept to returning participants. The activity starts by asking, "What do you think a conservator might be?" Given that most participants are unfamiliar with what a conservator does, this question becomes an opportunity for repeat visitors to share their previous knowledge with new groups. In addition to talking about conservation, the early learners are invited to engage with tools used in conservation work, and these activities are framed as part of their role as art doctors-in-training. As they observe demonstrations and participate using tools, they are introduced to new ideas on how artworks are cared for while encountering familiar household objects, such as a paintbrush, used in a new context, as well as less familiar tools, like an Optivisor or blunt-tipped tweezers. Discussing the overall concept of a conservator is also an opportunity to connect to the science and make the program more interdisciplinary.

In-Gallery Experience

With the idea of the conservator now in mind, the in-person participants are taken to the galleries. During this segment, groups have a chance to look closely at the art, both to learn about its history and cultural context as well as its conservation. The length of time in the gallery varies based on the children attending and travel time to and from the studio. To allow a flexible approach, we prepare a list of close-looking and movement-based activities that we can select based on the group's dynamic and the children's attention span. Adult participants also have their own unique needs and questions that emerge during the in-gallery experience. We find that it is useful to have multiple facilitators present for this section to be able to answer adult-level questions while keeping children engaged in activities.

The goal of the in-gallery experience is to encourage the children to look, observe, and make connections. Several questions and hands-on opportunities are designed for the in-gallery experience. During a previous workshop, we developed a program based on an NMAA special exhibition called *Secrets of the Lacquer Buddha*, which was held from 2017 to 2018 focusing on the technical study of three related Chinese Buddhas. This topic offered rich avenues for a conservation program, but the material needed to be adapted to three-to-eight-year-olds. During the in-gallery experience, the families were asked to compare the three sculptures in several different ways from a list of discussion prompts. During the sessions, we selected prompts from the list based on the group's dynamic and interests.

Art & Me: Solving Art Mysteries with Science

Secrets of the Lacquer Buddha In-gallery Prompts

- Close Looking: Ask participants to look to compare and contrast the Buddha sculptures.
- Weight: Encourage participants to guess how much the sculptures weigh. Do they think they weigh more or less than themselves? Show three materials that are the same size but different weights. One Buddha has a solid wood core, while the other two are hollow. As a result, the Buddhas are about the same size but different weights. Three disks were brought to the galleries for the children to hold that were made from Ethafoam, wood, and metal. The disks were the same size but very different weights, so it makes the idea more concrete.
- Materials: Encourage participants to find out what materials are used to make the sculptures. Show the case with materials in the front gallery. Provide samples of types of textiles for them to touch. Show pictures of textile fibers.
- Color: Ask participants to guess the original appearance of the sculptures and show image of reconstruction of a Buddha with colors "restored" to their original appearance.
- Thirty-second Look: Encourage visitors to look closer at the three-dimensional printed Buddhas in the front gallery using the magnifying glasses provided.

The in-gallery portion of the workshop also allows time for stories about conservation, an interactive opportunity to share information about the conservation and preservation of specific artworks.

Hands-on Art/Conservation Activity

After spending time in the gallery, the participants return to the classroom for the main activity that each group can do simultaneously. There also are several activity options for smaller groups available at the same time, sometimes we offer opportunities to reengage with starter activities, but often times we have new activities that build on what they just learned. Since older siblings are welcome to attend, this format provides engaging activities for a range of ages rather than just scaling one activity for everyone. When designing the main activity for a workshop, our goal is to make it scalable to all youth participants (Figure 3.1).

The projects are designed to be achievable for early learners but sometimes need some collaboration from their caregivers, especially for the youngest participants. For example, one project that relates ceramics and their damage by physical forces utilized the relatively well-known outreach

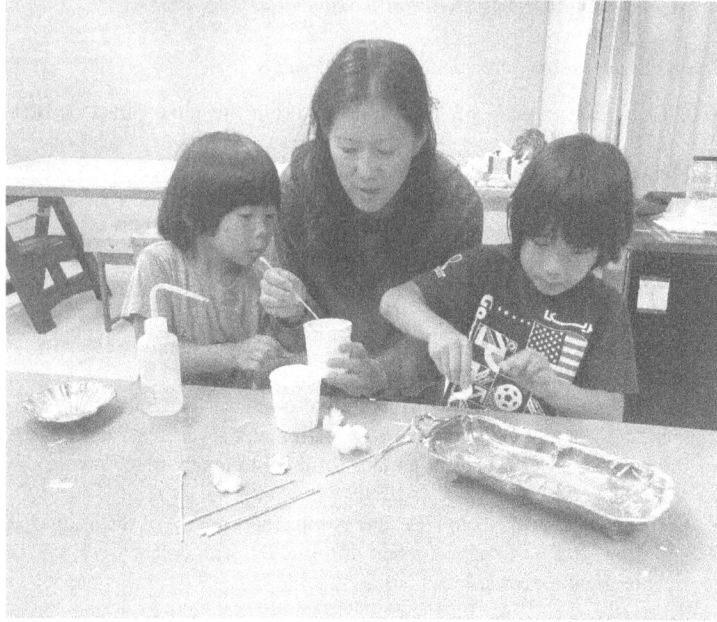

Figure 3.1 Family collaboration during an Art & Me activity with different aged participants.

Image courtesy of National Museum of Asian Art, Smithsonian Institution; photo by Ellen Chase.

activity of assembling pieces of a broken "ceramic." For this activity, we used printed images of pieces in the collections, preferably ones they just saw in the gallery. The images were mounted on foam or board and cut into several pieces. The pieces were cut in several ways with a range of options, extending from some with only a few pieces to some with multiple complicated sections to be joined together like a puzzle. Some of the most advanced activity packets included pieces missing from the object. The packets were distributed to participants based on age level and, if needed, children could step up from one packet set to a more advanced version.

As with the in-gallery portion of the program, we assess the participants' prior knowledge and adjust accordingly. For instance, we introduced the color wheel to prepare the children for an inpainting activity. In one session, most of the children knew about the color wheel, but in the next session, they didn't. In the latter case, we spent additional time to present the color wheel and allowed the participants to explore the ideas before moving on to the planned activities. Since there is a generous timeframe for in-person sessions, we account for in-depth explanations, like going over the color wheel with a group. In this way, we can complete all the planned portions of the session.

Art Doctor Conservation Report

Throughout every program, attendees are encouraged to practice close looking during the starter activities, in-gallery experiences, and main activity. This is an integral part of the workshop structure because we want to prepare participants when we introduce the concept of a condition examination report. For early learners, we provide a simplified condition report, referred to it as the Art Doctor Conservation Report. This report is included as a component of the main activity and provides an opportunity for families to consider and discuss deterioration, preservation, and preventive concerns relating to their project. Depending on the participants, we will sometimes lead a group discussion of the report and sometimes interact more individually with the children and their caregivers as they fill out the report.

The questions on the report consist of the following (Figure 3.2):

• Art Doctor/Conservator's Name
• Art's Name
• Examination

What three words best describe your artwork?
Circle which emoji best describes how you felt making your artwork. (emojis range from angry to happy)
What can you do to take care of your art?
Sketch the artwork you created.

The report is designed so that younger early learners work with their adult companions to fill out the questions, while those developing reading and writing skills can take a more active role if they wish. However, the drawing component of the report allows all of the participants an opportunity to actively engage with at least a portion of the report. While in some very specific instances we have made changes to this format, the sections of the Art Doctor Conservation Report remain the same for every session, providing consistency for repeat attendees and an opportunity to consider the questions for a new artwork.

Show-and-Tell

The in-person program format allows for informal opportunities to show one's work to program facilitators. As the groups work on their main activity, we actively facilitate the experience. When the program transitioned and was adapted for online audiences, this aspect of the program became more important as a means to interact with the participants as well as acknowledge and see their work.

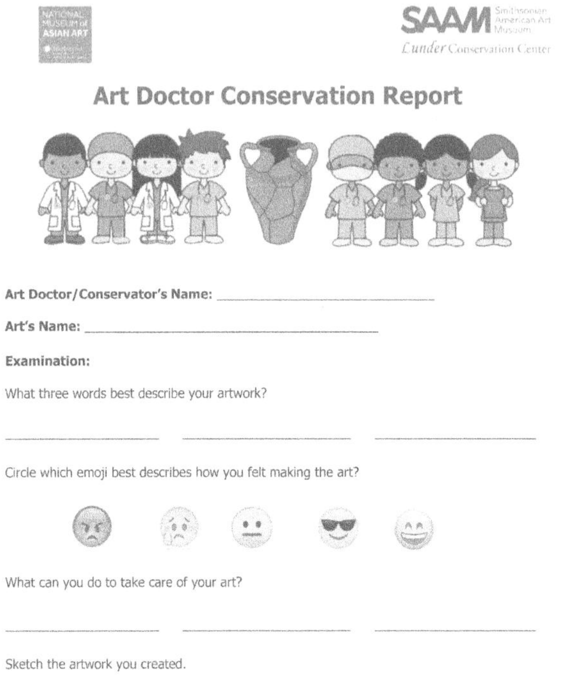

Figure 3.2 Art Doctor Conservation Report.

Image courtesy of National Museum of Asian Art and Smithsonian American Art Museum, Smithsonian Institution.

Take-Home Component

Each Art & Me workshop concludes with something tangible for the children to take home that will remind them of the experience and encourage further discussion and investigation. While we have many repeat attendees for the workshops, there are also many who only come once, so we hope to continue their exploration of cultural heritage conservation even if they are unable to attend another program. This can be a set of questions or a follow-up activity, but frequently, this component will be built into the project created during the workshop. For example, during the workshop about corrosion mentioned in Chapter 2, participants created a charm made from a silver disk that they could hang up (or if old enough, wear as a pendant). The children decorated the disks with a range of materials, such as stickers and rhinestones, but they also left a section uncovered. Essential to the project was a clear circular sticker applied to the surface of the metal so that it was covered, but the metal was visible beneath. The participants left with the task of watching what happens to the silver in both covered and uncovered areas. With take home components of the workshops, we suggest that everyone talk about what happens together at home, but we also encourage them to email us to let us know what they discovered.

Key to planning any activity with early learners is trying it out beforehand informally with willing families or on your own. This is particularly important for the take-home portion of the Art & Me program since it often relies on things developing over time. In one instance, the participants created identical prints of the same image. Then, we provided them with instructions to store one print in a folder and place the other in a window for one to two weeks. Before testing, we expected that the kid-friendly water-based printing ink would fade quickly, but we learned from our test samples that it was surprisingly resilient to light damage. We tested several other materials and decided to use tempera paint since it was still thick enough for printing but more sensitive to light fading. In addition to pre-workshop testing, we relied on trial and error in earlier sessions when we couldn't test supplies or activities with children in advance. During an early phase of the program, we used watercolor pencils during a workshop, thinking that it would help them practice their motor skills. However, the children struggled with the activity because they added too much water and created holes in the paper. This resulted in frustration on the part of the learners, making the main activity more challenging than it needed to be.

Art & Me Online Program Format

When switching to the online format of Art & Me due to the COVID-19 pandemic, the program shifted and evolved to best suit a digital platform. The online structure consists of a warm-up prompt, introduction of the role of an art conservator, exploration of the art collection related to the program topic, art activity, and art doctor report. Encouraging interaction in an online format has proven to be more challenging than in-person and required adjustments. We wanted to maintain the interactive nature of the in-person program while upholding the privacy of minors, the primary demographic of this program. Throughout each component of the online Art & Me workshops, the facilitators ask questions to which the caregivers type responses via the chat. To boost interaction, we moderate the chat by saying aloud the attendees' inquiries and answers. In addition to adding the virtual show-and-tell that we run to conclude the program, we shifted the order so that the art activity occurs before the collection exploration. This change has allowed participants to continue to create while we share conservation stories about museum collections. The online program includes reinforcement of the lesson objectives with follow-up activities and takeaway discussion questions.

Additionally, we compile the lesson resources in the Smithsonian Learning Lab, the Smithsonian Institution's free interactive content sharing platform. By adding resources, which include the slide deck, museum collection connections, and art project samples, the Learning Lab offering is a way to supplement, reinforce, and extend the virtual experience. These program refinements have boosted interaction and helped the program to cultivate a national and international audience.

Another major difference is that online workshops have no registration limit because participants cannot share their camera or unmute their microphone during sessions. This format allows us to protect the privacy of children while also limiting distractions. Participants can engage with presenters by using the chat functions available through Zoom webinar. While still a free program, we ask participants to pre-register in advance to receive webinar information and to provide them with a list of supplies. Unlike the in-person sessions, participants provide their own supplies. Taking this into account, we suggest low-cost supplies that are commonly kept at home or use recycled materials. These online sessions run for approximately forty-five minutes. This compressed timeframe is possible since participants actively engage in their art activity during the presentation of materials.

To best demonstrate an online Art & Me workshop, we have outlined a past program that delved into pest management.

Art & Me: Bugging Out

Warm-up Activity

The program began with participants, both children and caregivers, looking at six bug-related artworks from NMAA's and SAAM's collections and answering in the chat, "What do you see in these artworks? What does it make you wonder?" We welcomed participants to the program and moderated the Zoom chat throughout, the primary method of communication for attendees. For each session, we designate one staff member to be the chat moderator to encourage active participation throughout the program.

Introduction to Cultural Heritage Conservation

After the warm-up, welcome, and facilitators' introductions, we prompted participants to enter into the chat what they thought a conservator might be. We then asked participants to explore the image of an art conservator and pick out visual clues, such as gloves, a microscope, and cotton wool swabs, to demonstrate the role of a conservator. In each session, one of the conservators wears a lab coat and puts on gloves and an Optivisor to mirror the in-person experience of introducing the concept of an art doctor.

Art Activity

Then, we facilitated the art activity, sharing the supply list, which was emailed to all participants in the registration confirmation and event reminders. The materials were both age-appropriate and low-cost, allowing for substitutions in order to minimize barriers for the caregivers. Since Bugging Out was all about pest management, the art activity was making creepy crawlies out of different household items (egg carton, paper plate, cupcake liners, bottle caps, or popsicle sticks) and decorating them however the participants chose with paint, chenille stems, googly eyes, or pom-poms. Participants were encouraged to choose their favorite bug or to create a new one for their artwork. We demonstrated an example to help get participants started.

Conservation Stories

As participants continued to create, we shared conservation stories from each museum collection about bugs. We showed an art installation that used bugs at SAAM's Renwick Gallery as well as artists throughout time that have used insects to create special colors in their paint. We concluded this section with an introduction to pest mitigation, including Riley, the "Museum Dog," who sniffs out pests to protect art at the Museum of Fine Arts, Boston.

Art Doctor Conservation Report

We then went through the Art Doctor Conservation Report with the participants, modeling the creepy crawly sample artwork the Art & Me team created.

Show-and-Tell

We concluded the program with related questions for participants to consider after the program before moving into the participant show-and-tell. During this component, participants were asked to submit their artworks via email. We then pulled up the images of these artworks, discussed them, and connected them to the artworks featured in the workshop. After the program, we sent participants a feedback survey and direct link to the Smithsonian Learning Lab module with all the workshop teaching materials.

Chapter Takeaways

This chapter examined the various components of the Art & Me program and their interplay to create a multi-faceted experience for program participants. Key insights from the chapter include the significance of building a scientific component into programming, a comparison of the program in its in-person and virtual iterations, and the importance of post-workshop interactions to reinforce the learning experience.

Incorporating scientific elements in the different facets of the Art & Me program enables the presentation of conservation-related scientific concepts in approachable ways. Science and STEAM learning are incorporated to some extent into every aspect, from introductory activities that encourage close looking to the explanation of how to protect something in the Art Doctor Conservation Report. Our experience has shown that it is most effective when seamlessly integrated into the overall discussion while focusing on core concepts.

There are some key advantages and disadvantages of the in-person and virtual formats of the Art & Me program. Each format requires a unique approach to meet the needs of early learners and their caregivers effectively. As we offered this program, we learned that the length and sequence of the engagement needed to be adjusted. Additionally, opportunities for interaction and engagement are essential to keeping focus for either format but how that is done can differ greatly.

Although the move to virtual happened more rapidly and unexpectedly than anticipated, both formats have shown great promise, and we plan to continue in both formats. Based on the way our program is structured, however, we have decided to hold the two types of sessions separately rather than in a hybrid format in order to focus on the learner needs for each type of interaction.

Whether in person or online, structuring workshops with specific goals in mind not only makes them easier to plan but also makes them more accessible to the participants. While we focus on the concepts of connecting to art in the collections, agents of deterioration, and connecting to the lives of the children participating, there are certainly many other ways to approach introducing cultural heritage conservation to early learners. Each program will benefit from their own assessment of what they most want to convey to their audience during the initial planning phases. Also integral to planning is testing out all of the projects and activities to make sure they work as expected.

Additionally, for all cultural heritage preservation outreach to early learners, but particularly for those programs that may be only one session in length, it is well worth thinking about how to extend the workshop activities post-program to reinforce the experiences gained during the session. This can be as low tech as sending home a list of follow-up questions for attendees to discuss or tech-focused like sharing the online Smithsonian Learning Lab link with multiple digital resources to keep those thoughts and questions going.

Lastly, as with the development stage of Art & Me, formal and informal participant feedback continues to be a key factor in improving and evolving the sessions. While the more formal component will be discussed in Chapter 4, informal feedback often happens in real-time for both virtual and in-person formats and can be as simple as the questions or comments from participants during a workshop or noticing wandering attention spans during an activity.

Even limited feedback can be essential to help craft and develop programming for any audiences, especially for early learners.

Notes

1 Beyond the Art & Me program, the Department of Conservation and Scientific Research (CSR) at the National Museum of Asian Art combines art and science in all of its work. The staff includes several full-time research scientists as well as conservators. See the CSR section of the NMAA website for additional information (NMAA n.d.).
2 As we developed the Art & Me program, we were inspired by the work of Ron Ritchart. In *Creating Cultures of Thinking: The 8 Forces We Must Master to Truly Transform Our Schools* (Ritchart 2015), he refers to the language of identity as instances where learners take on the identities of scientists, writers, mathematicians, or artists in order to put them in closer proximity to the subject matter. Learners take an active role in the learning process and develop a deeper connection to the materials and concepts presented.

References

NMAA (National Museum of Asian Art). n.d. "Conservation." Accessed 12 October, 2023: https://asia.si.edu/explore-art-culture/interactives/peacock-room/conservation/.
Ritchart, Ron. 2015. *Creating Cultures of Thinking: The 8 Forces We Must Master to Truly Transform Our Schools*. San Fransisco: Jossey-Bass.

4 Building Evaluative Capacity for Conservation Outreach Programs

Ellen Chase, Laura Hoffman, and Matthew Lasnoski

Introduction

Although there has been an increase in conservation outreach programs for school-aged children, challenges still exist in evaluating these efforts for cultural institutions due to limited resources, a need for training on how to analyze data, and time constraints (AIC 2022, 1). Using these challenges as a starting point, this chapter provides resources and shares first-hand experience on building capacity for evaluation of new conservation outreach programs in the hopes of encouraging future visitor studies on cultural heritage outreach programs.

Both informal and formal evaluation methods are effective tools to approach assessment of conservation outreach efforts. These methods can help determine whether programs are achieving their intended goals and resources are being used efficiently. Evaluative research efforts can be embedded in every stage of the program from planning to implementation. By incorporating assessment throughout the program's lifecycle, educators and conservators can use iterative refinement to help programs grow and evolve to better meet the needs of their audiences. According to the American Institute for Conservation K-12 Outreach Programs Survey, program organizers often face tough decisions on how to allocate time and resources to create a sustainable model for consistent outreach, and insights from data can be applied to guide the evolution of outreach initiatives (AIC 2022, 1).

Building Internal Capacity for Audience Research

Even with limited experience in audience research, there are practical and meaningful steps that anyone can take to understand their audience's needs and motivations. It is important to remember that although a visitor study requires a systematic approach to data collection and analysis, there is still virtue in informally gathering feedback from visitors to learn about their experience as a first step. Even talking to a handful of participants will help build

DOI: 10.4324/9781003333210-5

comfort gathering the responses and will provide a team with more information about their audience than before.

For the Art & Me program, we started small and built our capacity for evaluation over time. From experience, the program team learned that it was valuable to begin with an informal survey and conduct informal interviews with caregivers to gather input during the pilot phase. This allowed the team to gain hands-on experience, build confidence in new skills, and gradually learn about what worked in workshops from the audience's perspective.

Some research methods will require additional training to build internal capacity or hiring external evaluators depending on a team's prior experience and knowledge. For more complex visitor and participant studies, program staff may need to create partnerships and obtain institutional resources. Depending on budget and staff interest, pursuing professional development opportunities and hiring external evaluation experts can accelerate building evaluative capacity.[1]

Choosing Evaluative Methods for Intergenerational Audiences

Depending on the program's goals and objectives, the first step is to define research questions and then determine how to measure progress toward the desired outcomes.[2] In these initial stages, the team should utilize the resources already available. Accessing and incorporating existing knowledge and data can be used to inform the development of research questions that the team seeks to answer through evaluation. Using the Smithsonian's Art & Me program as an example, the program team was most interested in measuring how satisfied participants were with the program, what kinds of learning took place, and what could be improved to meet the audience's needs.

In the context of youth and family programming, it is essential to consider the unique perspectives and needs of all members of the intergenerational unit (Cromartie, Kwon, and Welch 2021, 2–3). There are additional guidelines and protections for collecting information on children from the Institutional Review Board (IRB).[3] Taking these protocols into consideration, it is possible to develop age-appropriate methods for gathering informal feedback directly from children. One approach used by the Art & Me program team is to incorporate play and creativity when collecting information from young learners. Throughout the program, we ask questions about their experience and what is being learned to assess how they are interacting with the content. During instruction, we use language that encourages collaboration and conversation between caregivers and learners. Writing down observations, taking pictures, and taking notes are ways to document the learning process that can be used later when reflecting on the program and trying to determine what improvements can be made. This type of feedback from youth audiences can support and build on data collected in formal evaluative studies administered to caregivers.

When age appropriate, asking all participants to engage in reflective activities can be insightful, since the feedback comes directly from their perspective (Reggio Emilia Approach n.d.; Harvard University n.d.). One can engage with visual aids, symbols, and open-ended questions to ask young learners to share their experience. This will allow them to express what they enjoyed and found challenging in the lesson.

There are several formal evaluation methods that can be used to assess the program from the caregiver's perspective:

Focus Groups

Focus groups are a more in-depth way to gather feedback from participants. The program team can select a small group of participants and have a facilitator guide a discussion around specific topics related to the program. This method may be more effective if one has an established program with repeat participants willing to participate. This group could help guide a program through a transition period using their prior knowledge of the program and be used to get their buy-in on future changes (American Alliance of Museums 2022).

Observations

This method can be used to evaluate the program in action. The team can observe participants during the program to see how engaged they are, how well they are following instructions, and what challenges they may be facing. This information is helpful for observing young learners who cannot participate in surveys and other formal evaluation methods.

Exit Interviews

Exit interviews are a way to gather feedback from participants as they leave the program. The team can ask participants about what they enjoyed the most, what they learned, and what they would change about the program. It is best to keep these conversations brief, open-ended, and focused on caregivers sharing what they found most satisfying (University of Kansas n.d.).

Surveys

Teams can use online survey tools or paper forms that can be distributed either onsite or via email after the program has ended. Survey questions should be clear and concise. Visitors have limited time and attention, and a survey should not take the average respondent more than five minutes nor be longer than fifteen questions according to the United States Office of Management and Budget.[4]

When selecting appropriate evaluative tools, it is important to align the chosen methods to the program's goals and objectives. As discussed, starting small and focusing on learning about one aspect of the program would be a strategic decision that can help build institutional capacity for collecting visitor feedback more sustainably (Renger and Hurley 2006). A critical consideration is what types of data will resonate with stakeholders and help drive decision-making. In the case of the Art & Me program, we developed an exit survey following the pilot program to measure progress within the program. The survey allowed us to track responses over time and collect both qualitative and quantitative data for reporting purposes (see Appendix A).

Generating Insights from Participant Feedback

Although data analysis from formal visitor studies requires specialized training in statistics and human subjects research methods, there are still worthwhile actions that a beginner can take to improve their offerings and to learn from their audiences. As a starting point, consistently reviewing data on a regular schedule builds a habit of integrating visitor feedback into decision-making. Using the Art & Me program as an example, we would meet the week after workshops to share observations and any other feedback to frame how to improve the program offerings. These informal meetings allowed the team to reflect on our work while prioritizing the participants' perspectives.

In addition to identifying a program's strengths, audience research will undoubtedly uncover pain points and areas for improvement. When these are uncovered, it is important to identify the most critical problems that have the highest impact on the participant experience.[5] Changes are scalable to institutional priorities and needs, and some feedback might require collaboration between departments and partners to resolve. Additionally, staff can monitor and measure the impact of changes over time with continued evaluation by asking the same questions and using the initial results as a baseline for future improvement.

Building Evaluative Capacity for Smithsonian's Art & Me Program (2016 to 2023)

Background

Learning about the Art & Me audience evolved incrementally over time as the program matured. In the early pilot phase, we provided informal opportunities for caregivers and youth to write their responses about what they learned or what surprised them in workshops. This direct audience feedback allowed us to make changes to the program structure as we learned what resonated with participants. Shortly after pilot workshops, we met to review observations, written responses, and photographs to discuss improvements and ideas for future workshops. Dedicating time for reflection and discussion was critical for the future growth of the program. At this early stage, we did not have training to conduct a full-scale visitor study but were able to iterate on the offerings and make improvements.

To receive sustained funding and institutional support, it was necessary to evaluate the outreach to demonstrate Art & Me's effectiveness and determine what benefits early learners and their caregivers received from the program. We developed a survey for Art & Me that was able to measure the audience's experience and satisfaction in a more systematic way. At the National Museum of Asian Art (NMAA), newly trained evaluators supported the development and implementation of the survey. Having in-house trained evaluators provided the program team with the ability to pull from a bank of existing questions and compare results across other programs and exhibition offerings when analyzing the results of the survey.[6]

Art & Me Survey Background

When the Art & Me program started in 2016, the data collected from participants was intended to help improve the program offering, and there were no plans to share the results publicly. As a result, these initial evaluations were not submitted to the IRB, and as such, the specific data cannot be used in the following discussion. When the program expanded to include the Smithsonian American Art Museum (SAAM) three years later, a new survey was developed that was approved by the IRB. Since then, program facilitators collected 150 surveys from September 2019 to April 2023, and data collection for the survey is ongoing (see Appendix A). Seven core questions from the survey are the focus of the remainder of this chapter in order to demonstrate a list of basic questions that can be utilized and built upon to expand visitor studies for conservation outreach for youth audiences.

In the current sample of eighteen workshops that can be included, the Art & Me program has served 245 intergenerational groups, comprised of approximately 1045 individuals. Most of these workshops were held online with fifteen online workshops and three in-person workshops. One caregiver per family was asked to complete the survey, and 61% of participants completed surveys following the workshop.

Visitor Learning and Experience

In this section, three audience experience measures are discussed: Overall Experience Rating (OER), Satisfying Experiences, and Surprise. This discussion of the survey results serves as an introduction to why these measures are used to understand participants' experiences and the importance of evaluating cultural heritage conservation outreach efforts.

Overall Experience Rating

To measure the quality of visitor experience, the Smithsonian Institution and many other museums across the United States utilize the Overall Experience Rating (OER) scale. The rating scale options are Poor, Fair, Good, Excellent, and Outstanding. This measure is designed to provide a holistic understanding of a visitor's experience, and it is typically placed at the beginning of a survey. Past studies using the OER scale indicate visitors who rate their experience as Poor, Fair, or Good often have some degree of criticism. For analytical purposes, these three categories are grouped together and designated as "Less than Excellent." Respondents who rate their experience Excellent are satisfied by their visit, while those who rate their experience as Outstanding encounter a level of satisfaction where Excellent is no longer adequate to describe the quality of their experience (Pekarik, Schreiber, and Visscher 2018). By including an Outstanding category, program facilitators can identify and understand moments that exceed the audience's expectations.

The Art & Me program survey includes the OER as a holistic experience measure to track the quality of visitor experience over time. From 2019 to 2023, 50% of respondents rated their experience as Outstanding, 39% rated their experience as Excellent, and 11% rated their experience as Less than Excellent. At NMAA, the OER is used across all public programs and exhibitions, which allows the museum staff to contextualize visitor experience across all its offerings. In the same way, as evaluating conservation outreach programs expands, data sharing agreements between programs using the same survey questions, such as the OER, could provide better insights into these results and yield data-based strategies to enhance conservation outreach programs.

Satisfying Experiences

As a follow-up question to the OER scale, program facilitators can dig deeper into their audience's experience by including a measure for satisfying experiences. In the Art & Me survey, participants are asked to select from seven satisfying experiences: (1) to have fun and be entertained, (2) to learn something new or feel intellectually stimulated, (3) to socialize or to be with friends and family, (4) to relax and slow down, (5) to feel inspired or admire things that are beautiful, (6) to have a new experience, and (7) to give friends or family an enjoyable experience. The order of the seven satisfying experiences is randomized in the survey to avoid bias toward earlier answers (Blair, Imai, and Zhou 2015). Program participants are allowed to mark as many satisfying experiences as are relevant to them.

The question is designed to understand the range of positive experiences caregivers and youth experienced in the workshop. For the Art & Me program, the satisfying experiences were selected from a broader list used for other public programs and exhibitions. When the Art & Me survey started, all NMAA public programs measured the same satisfying experiences for comparative purposes. While integrating this question into a survey, the team should choose satisfying experiences that are most appropriate to their research and institutional needs.

Five of the seven satisfying experiences (all except for feeling relaxed and socializing with family and friends) were reported by more than half of the Art & Me participants. Figure 4.1 provides the percentage of participants who were satisfied by each experience ranked from highest to lowest. Over two-thirds of attendees selected learning something new as a satisfying experience, the highest of all the satisfying experience categories.

Surprise

The Art & Me survey included a question that prompted program participants to report if anything surprised them during the workshop, and 54% of respondents were surprised by some aspect of the workshop. Participants who rated their experience as Outstanding had a significantly higher likelihood of reporting being surprised during the workshop.[7] As seen in Figure 4.2, 73% of respondents who rated their experience as Outstanding also felt surprised. For respondents who did not rate their experience as Outstanding, only 35%

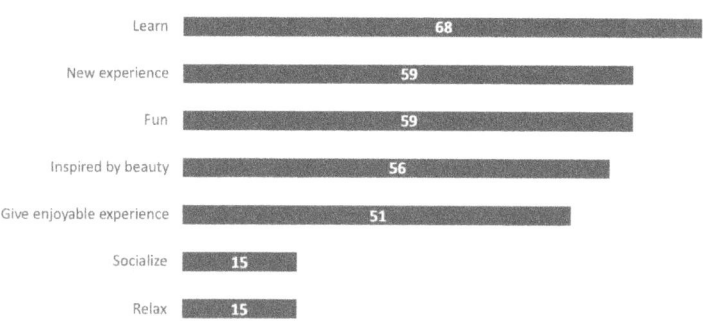

Figure 4.1 Art & Me satisfying experiences (in percent).

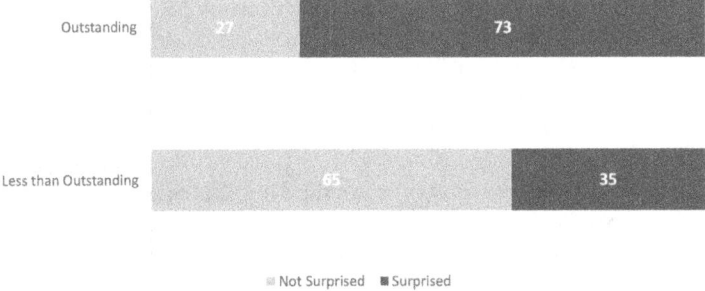

Figure 4.2 Surprise by OER (in percent).

reported feeling surprised. This finding suggests that surprise can provide insights into what contributes to an Outstanding participant experience.

In the survey, the respondents who marked that they were surprised were prompted to provide additional information in the form of an open-ended response. The seventy unique comments from respondents fall broadly into two categories: Museum Conservation and Collections, as well as Interactivity and Creating.

Museum Conservation and Collections

The most mentioned surprises in the open-ended responses were related to the museum's collection and learning about museum conservation practices. Many respondents mentioned specific details about objects featured in sessions, such as writing on oracle bones from Ancient China and how bug specimens are preserved in artworks. Even more common is being surprised about how objects are preserved in museums and learning about a conservator's job.

Participant responses include:

- My son loved becoming an art doctor in-training. Museums rarely show how work happens behind-the-scenes.
- The information about protecting artwork from weather. I somehow had never thought of the need for that.
- She gained a first understanding of the work that goes on 'behind the scenes' at a museum.
- I really like the conservation angle this program took; you don't find that in museum programs. It's especially neat how it was given an early-ish education lens.
- We loved the behind-the-scenes experience of working at a museum!

Interactivity and Creating

Program participants also expressed surprise regarding the interactive nature of the workshops and their ability to participate and create themselves. Respondents mentioned the ability of participants to choose their level of engagement and pride in the artworks they created.
Participant responses include:

- The quality of the project even using simple items we already had at home! My kids are wanting to create more with the soap carvings!
- I was positively surprised how engaging the event was. My daughter was really interested and proudly showed her artwork to the whole family afterwards.
- That the children enjoyed working with the hands-on tools as much as they did.
- It is always a joy to see the museum's art collection as well as the artwork that the participants create at the end.

Visitor Context

The Importance of Demographic Data

In addition to experience-based questions, the Art & Me survey included questions that captured audience demographics and behaviors. Including demographic information in a survey can provide insights into who is participating in the program, their backgrounds, and experiences.
Demographic information can be critical in:

Improving Program Effectiveness

Demographic information can help the program team understand who is participating in their program and identify any gaps in participation. For example, if a program is intended for families with young children but is primarily attended by children outside the age range, the team can use demographic information to identify this discrepancy and adjust their program accordingly.

Tailoring Programs to Specific Audiences

Demographic information can also help program facilitators tailor programs to specific audiences. For example, if a program is intended for low-income families, demographic information can help facilitators understand the barriers and challenges to design programs that are more effective in meeting their needs.

Applying for External Funding

Many grants and other funding sources require demographic information to ensure that programs are reaching target audiences. Including demographic information in surveys can help program facilitators demonstrate that their programs are meeting the needs of underserved populations.

Sharing with Key Stakeholders

Demographic information can also be useful for sharing information with key stakeholders, such as board members, donors, and community leaders. Sharing demographic information can help stakeholders understand who is participating in programs and how programs are meeting the needs of different communities.

Privacy concerns can arise when collecting demographic information, especially if it includes sensitive information such as race, ethnicity, or income. To address these concerns, it is important to inform participants about why the information is being collected, how it will be used, and how it will be protected. Participants should have the option to decline to answer any demographic questions, and the information should be stored securely and used only for its intended purposes. Additionally, when reporting demographic data, it is important to aggregate the data to protect individual privacy and avoid the identification of specific participants (HHS (United States Department of Health and Human Services) n.d.). In general, a good rule of thumb is to collect only the demographic data that is necessary to meet your objectives.

Demographic Data

Age

The Art & Me survey asked the adult participants to identify their age in twelve distinct categories in five-year increments except for ages eighteen to nineteen and seventy and over. Over half (51%) of participants surveyed were between thirty-five and forty-four.

Historically, the program team has used this data to show that adults coming to these intergenerational programs are varied and diverse. Although many are within the typical parenting age, the findings suggest that older siblings, guardians, childcare providers, or grandparents bring young children to Art & Me as well. In our programs, we use inclusive language like "caregiver" and "adult companion" to acknowledge the variety of relationships.

Prior to 2019, we collected the age of children in the programs in the survey, and we have transitioned to collecting the information in pre-registration so that we can collect the age of all children as opposed to a sample provided by the survey. We learned that older siblings, primarily ages six to eight, were also participating in Art & Me. Based on these findings, we expanded the age range from ages three to five to ages three to eight and scaled the complexity of projects targeted at older siblings.

Residence

Through all four Art & Me survey versions, adult participants were asked to state whether they live in the United States or another country. If they selected the United States, the participant was asked to provide their zip code. According to the survey, 89% of participants lived in the United States, while 11% attended the program from another country. Among US residents, 45% of participants lived outside the Washington Metropolitan area, demonstrating the program's reach beyond local audiences. International participants primarily came from Canada and the United Kingdom. Prior to offering the Art & Me program online, the program did not reach participants outside of the Washington, DC, area in any meaningful way. The increased reach of the program has been one of the reasons the program team has continued to offer programs online.

Visitation Frequency

Since the Art & Me program transitioned to include an online format, attendees were asked if they ever attended an online public program at the Smithsonian Institution. Over the past three years, Art & Me attracted more first-time visitors (55%) than repeat visitors (45%) for its online workshops. When the Art & Me program was first conceived, the Public Programs team sought to bring in a new audience with this program, and the survey data indicates that this occurred. There is, however, a significant number of attendees who have been to previous programs as well. These repeat visitors are important because they suggest that the content is varied and that it is worth coming back again.

Understanding the ratio of first-time to repeat visitors has helped us gauge the program's ability to attract and retain participants, indicating its appeal and relevance. By tracking this information, the team has been able to identify patterns and trends, enabling us to tailor our offerings and experiences to cater to the specific needs and interests of the audience. In Chapter 3, the introduction to cultural heritage conservation section of an Art & Me workshop is an example of how content is tailored to provide both consistent foundational information for first-time participants and customized content throughout for repeat visitors.

How Participants Heard about Art & Me

Program participants were also asked how they heard about the Art & Me workshops in all the survey versions. The question was adapted based on onsite and online programs (see Appendix A). For the online programs, Art & Me participants chose between the following options: Smithsonian Museum website, word of mouth, advertisement or sponsored post, news story/article, online event or activity listing, Smithsonian Museum print or e-newsletter, or social media. For onsite programs, there were additional choices, such as the information desk or wandering by, which are only possible for onsite visits. Participants were able to select multiple ways in which they heard about the workshop and could write in other ways that were not provided in the list.

The top three ways individuals heard about events were online event or activity listing (36%), Smithsonian Museum website (22%) and the Smithsonian Museum print or e-newsletter (22%), as seen in Figure 4.3. These findings were shared with the Marketing and Communications department and informed the promotion plan for upcoming workshops.

Art & Me Survey Analysis

The survey findings indicate that the most satisfying experience for program participants was learning, and visitor comments reflect their surprise and appreciation for the program's structured format, learning about "behind-the-scenes" museum practice, and engaging activities.

These findings suggest that outreach programs like Art & Me can be an effective approach to achieving education on sustainable cultural heritage principles among our youngest learners. Moreover, the survey results indicate that audiences are built over time, and participants are likely to

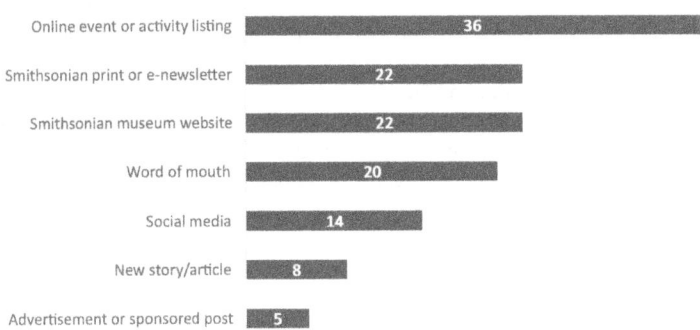

Figure 4.3 Online programs: how did you hear about this program? (in percent).

remain faithful to programs that engage them in a structured format. The Art & Me program's approach of combining interactive activities with learning reinforces the participants' memory and makes the learning process enjoyable.

Chapter Takeaways

For museum professionals looking to start or build on their program evaluation, starting small and gathering baselines to learn about an audience rather than fixating on setting and hitting specific targets from the outset makes the process less formidable. It is important to establish a starting point and gradually improve the program based on the insights gained. Any result, whether positive or not, is useful because it provides direction for improving your offering. By regularly evaluating the program's impact and adjusting strategies accordingly, professionals can iteratively refine and strengthen their outreach efforts.

The Art & Me program demonstrates the merit of employing both qualitative and quantitative methods in evaluation. Quantitative data, such as demographic measures, provides insights into the characteristics of the program's participants, enabling program teams to understand their audience better. On the other hand, qualitative methods, such as open-ended responses gathered in surveys or during activities, allow for a deeper understanding of the participant's experience, capturing their thoughts, feelings, and impressions. Both types of data are essential for gaining a comprehensive understanding of the program's effectiveness and improving the participant experience.

The survey findings suggest that engaging young learners in a structured format that combines interactive activities with learning can be an effective approach to achieving education on sustainable cultural heritage principles. As we continue to face challenges in the preservation of our cultural heritage, it is essential to engage and inspire the next generation of cultural stewards, and outreach programs like Art & Me provide an excellent opportunity to do so.

For those eager to develop their evaluation skills, engaging in professional development opportunities can be immensely beneficial. Investing in training and expanding one's knowledge in areas, such as evaluation methodologies, data analysis, and program design, can enhance the ability to assess and improve outreach programs effectively. Additionally, networking with other professionals in the field and participating in conferences and workshops can provide valuable insights and inspire new approaches to audience research and evaluation. With increased evaluation of conservation outreach for early learners, additional visitor studies about the skills children acquire and the effectiveness of STEAM-based pedagogy could produce helpful findings to inform the future of outreach efforts.

Notes

1 The Visitor Studies Association (VSA) is committed to offering year-round professional development opportunities for its members and other individuals looking to further their professional expertise in the field of visitor studies in museums, zoos, nature centers, visitor centers, historic sites, parks, and other informal learning settings. See Visitor Studies Association, "Professional Development" (Visitor Studies Association n.d.).

2 For a guide on how to approach setting goals, see Robert Stein, "Becoming a Data Startup – Part III Goals" (Stein 2017).

3 The guidelines are primarily geared toward human subjects research in the United States. For more information, see US Department of Health and Human Services, "Research with Children FAQs" (HHS n.d.).

4 The US Office of Management and Budget publishes guidance for federal agencies, like the Smithsonian, that provides direction on parameters for surveys. See Office of Management and Budget, "Section 280 – Managing Customer Experience and Improving Service Delivery" (OMB (United States Office of Management and Budget) 2022).

5 Human-centered design methods can be helpful for improving visitor offerings. For advice on prioritizing services improvements, see Susan Farrell, "UX Research Cheat Sheet" (Farrell 2017).

6 Staff who support audience research projects need to be certified in human subjects research. For more information on certification, see CITI Program, "Human Subjects Research (HSR)" (CITI Program n.d.).

7 A chi-square test was conducted to examine the relationship between an outstanding rating and surprise during a workshop. The test yielded a chi-squared value of 15.715 with 1 degree of freedom and a p-value of 0.00007363, which are considered to be statistically significant.

References

American Alliance of Museums. 2022. "Conducting Focus Groups." October 14, 2022. https://www.aam-us.org/wire/ku/conducting-focus-groups/.

AIC (American Institute for Conservation). 2022. "Conservation K-12 Outreach Programs Survey." January 12, 2022. https://www.culturalheritage.org/docs/default-source/publications/reports/survey-reports/conservation-k-12-outreach-programs-survey-report.pdf?sfvrsn=3eca1520_4.

Blair, Graeme, Kosuke Imai, and Yang-Yang Zhou. 2015. "Design and Analysis of the Randomized Response Technique." *Journal of the American Statistical Association* 110, no. 511: 1305–1306. https://doi.org/10.1080/01621459.2015.1050028.

CITI Program. n.d. "Human Subjects Research." Accessed 10 November, 2023. https://about.citiprogram.org/series/human-subjects-research-hsr/.

Cromartie, Nicole, Kyong-Ah Kwon, and Meghan Welch. 2021. *Evaluating Early Learning in Museums: Planning for Our Youngest Visitors*. London: Routledge. https://doi.org/10.4324/9780429340413.

Farrell, Susan. 2017. "UX Research Cheat Sheet." Nielsen Norman Group. February 12, 2017. https://www.nngroup.com/articles/ux-research-cheat-sheet/.

Harvard University, Graduate School of Education. "Project Zero's Thinking Routine Toolbox." Accessed 1 July, 2023. https://pz.harvard.edu/thinking-routines.

HHS (United States Department of Health and Human Services). n.d. "Research with Children FAQs." Accessed 1 July, 2023. https://www.hhs.gov/ohrp/regulations-and-policy/guidance/faq/children-research/index.html.

———. 2020. "OHRP Guidance on Elimination of IRB Review of Research Applications and Proposals." Last updated July 20, 2020. https://www.hhs.gov/ohrp/regulations-and-policy/guidance/elimination-of-irb-review-of-research-applications-and-proposals/index.html.

OMB (United States Office of Management and Budget). 2022. "Section 280 – Managing Customer Experience and Improving Service Delivery." Accessed 1 July, 2023. https://www.performance.gov/cx/assets/files/2022-OMB-Circular-A11-Section-280.pdf.

Pekarik, Andrew, James Schreiber, and Nick Visscher. 2018. "Overall Experience Rating – Measuring Visitor Responses in Museums." *Curator: The Museum Journal* 61 (2): 353–365.

Renger, Ralph, and Carolyn Hurley. 2006. "From Theory to Practice: Lessons Learned in the Application of the ATM Approach to Developing Logic Models." *Evaluation and Program Planning* 29 (2): 106–119. https://doi.org/10.1016/j.evalprogplan.2006.01.004.

Reggio Emilia Approach. n.d. "Values." Accessed 1 July, 2023. https://www.reggiochildren.it/en/reggio-emilia-approach/valori-en/.

Stein, Robert. 2017. "Becoming a Data Startup – Part III Goals." *Alliance Blog*. American Alliance of Museums. May 17, 2017. https://www.aam-us.org/2017/05/30/becoming-a-data-startup-part-iii-goals/.

University of Kansas. n.d. Center for Community Health and Development "Section 12: Conducting Interviews." The Community Toolbox. Accessed 8 August, 2023. https://ctb.ku.edu/en/table-of-contents/assessment/assessing-community-needs-and-resources/conduct-interviews/main.

Visitor Studies Association. n.d. "Professional Development." Accessed 10 November, 2023. https://visitorstudies.org/professional-development.

Part II

Engagement with Early Learners in Different Environments

The Smithsonian Institution's Art & Me program serves as just one example of how one might create opportunities for early learners to experience cultural heritage conservation. Part II of this book consists of six case studies to serve as inspiration, or at least as a place to begin, to encourage others to adopt outreach programs for early learners. Although Part II does not endeavor to encompass every geographical region, it showcases a diverse range of case studies from Lebanon, Norway, Singapore, the United Kingdom, and the United States. This compilation facilitates comparisons of varied approaches and circumstances, which acknowledges that not everyone has access to the same resources or museum collections. Our intention is to provide readers with a range of scenarios where outreach for early learners can thrive. With much of the world becoming hybrid, we also consider online outreach and how both virtual and in-person programming can provide unique and complementary components to effectively introduce the importance of cultural heritage and its preservation to young children.

Each of these studies focuses on an example of guided learning, in part because, as discussed in earlier chapters, this approach has shown to be effective for engaging early learners. Additionally, at the time of starting this book, this was the most established mechanism for reaching the early learner audience. The field is constantly evolving, however, and even as we write this book, more self-guided models, such as exhibitions, books, and online resources, for this age group are now available and could be examined in future publications.

Additionally, it is important to note that all the contributors of this book, including educators and conservators, primarily work or are trained in the cultural heritage sector. While the perspectives of classroom teachers are not included in this volume, it opens an avenue for future publications to integrate insights from educators working within formal school settings.

The case studies consider different contexts for outreach, and they progress in order from an informal family day at a museum in Carmarthen, Wales, in Chapter 5 to more formal learning structures, culminating in a full set of online teacher resources from the Michael C. Carlos Museum

DOI: 10.4324/9781003333210-6

in Atlanta, Georgia, in Chapter 10. While some case studies consider one-time events, such as the American University of Beirut Archaeological Museum's glass conservation program discussed in Chapter 7, others present more long-term opportunities, like the afterschool program at an International Baccalaureate school in Norway, where children are introduced to conservation over several sessions in Chapter 9.

In most cases, conservators and scientists collaborate with educators, and we hope to show that this is not as complicated as it sounds. While the Cleveland Museum of Art, who presents their Art to Go program in Chapter 8, has a long-standing collaboration between museum educators and conservators, other case studies highlight first-time collaborations. Furthermore, the case studies provide examples of different ways to generate a program, from creating a program from scratch to modifying existing programs to fit early learners, as well as the evolution of a more informal one-time program into a more extensive ongoing series as presented in Chapter 6 by the Heritage Conservation Centre in Singapore.

While the case studies in this section of the book follow a general guided format, each is written from the authors' specific perspectives and with their individual voices. Despite the differences between the programs discussed in these case studies, all of the authors have the common thread of seeing the universal potential of preservation education for the littlest stewards of cultural heritage.

5   Low Cost, High Fun

Creating a Playful Conservation Activity Day

Jenny Mathiasson

Introduction

My work as a private practice conservator has almost always been people-centered: outreach and sharing the profession with others is core to my practice. Since 2014, I have been working with children and young people whenever opportunity presents itself. It led me to do a Heritage Learning course in 2015, and I worked closely with teachers, homeschool groups, and education staff for four years to put collections care on the curriculum in Yorkshire. What we do in conservation and museums is genuinely interesting to people and building an understanding of what we do from an early age is so important. The following is a case study from my recent work in Wales, which is where I am now based.

Haf o Hwyl (Summer of Fun)

During the summer of 2022, Carmarthenshire County Council Museums Service (now CofGâr) kindly invited me to lead an activity day that was part of *Haf o Hwyl* (Summer of Fun), a bilingual event program paid for by the Welsh government in conjunction with the Federation of Museums and Art Galleries of Wales.

The program aimed to provide free and enriching activities for children and young people from birth to age twenty-five to help support their well-being in some way between July 1 and September 30, 2022. In the program's second year, its primary objectives were to give the target audience a chance to express themselves through creative fun and play with friends and peers.

The museum had asked for a day themed around conservation and collections care with hands-on activities. Because of the museum service policies around safeguarding, no children would be left unsupervised with the facilitators, so we knew we had to be able to engage both the caregivers and kids. Activities would need to be easily adaptable to a wide range of ages and

DOI: 10.4324/9781003333210-7

levels of understanding, so finding the right facilitators to allow that flexibility would be essential.

All printed materials, such as signs or instructions, had to be provided in Welsh and English. The museum had no dedicated learning staff at the time, which was part of the reason for creating partnerships with conservators. Fortunately, my experience developing activities alongside teachers, museum educators, and caregivers meant I felt confident creating a fun day focused on conservation and play.

What's a Conservator? Explaining the Profession

My first challenge was to explain what conservators even do. I had to assume that adults and children alike were likely unaware of the profession.

Storytelling can be a powerful tool, and museum professionals should be bold in using both stories and analogies when talking about conservation and cultural heritage. While kids can dazzle us with their sometimes-unexpected appreciation of nuance, it is always a good idea to find something with ideas and concepts that are relatable to them. All young children in Wales have visited a doctor, dentist, or nurse in their lifetime, so I've taken to telling them that a conservator is a doctor for things rather than people.

The questions are immediate: what's a hospital for things like? Can things get sick or injured? Can they be made better? Do you use bandages? Is there an ambulance for things? These questions are jumping-off points where improvised storytelling and invitations for more questions are possible.

What Makes a Fun Day Out? Choosing Activities

After introducing the concept of an art conservator, I selected activities that highlighted key aspects of our work. Since many of our day-to-day activities can be a little risky, I knew I would likely have to simulate a lot of what we do in a safe way for our audiences and collection objects.

Activities needed to be conservation-focused, fun, safe, and thrifty. They also needed to be low on the messiness scale given that the event was held in two museum galleries. That's not to say the activities did not create any mess; instead, it was about an agreed amount and type of mess alongside buy-in for thorough clean-up afterwards. For example, paint or adhesive was considered too risky as it could have damaged the floors of the galleries or potentially have splashed onto walls or cases with the over-enthusiastic flick of a brush. However, colored pencils and fake dust in the form of potato flour did not carry that same risk so were okay to use. I also eliminated options that were too expensive or that had limited reusability, as I wanted these to be repeatable and portable for future occasions.

The final list comprised eight activities:

Guessing the Tool Bags

A tactile activity in which small conservation tools or supplies (such as a piece of smoke sponge or a short-handled brush) were put inside an opaque sealed bag that could be kneaded or felt for shape and texture (Figure 5.1). I used food-grade coffee bags for mine and kept the same type of tools and supplies on the bench along with some additional supplies for visual inspiration.

Reconstructing a Ceramic

An interactive station with pre-broken terracotta pots in five to eight pieces and tape to hold these together when reconstructed (avoiding adhesives). The activity could be made more challenging by removing one of the pieces before the child had a go. The pots came from my garden and had begun to crack due to frost.

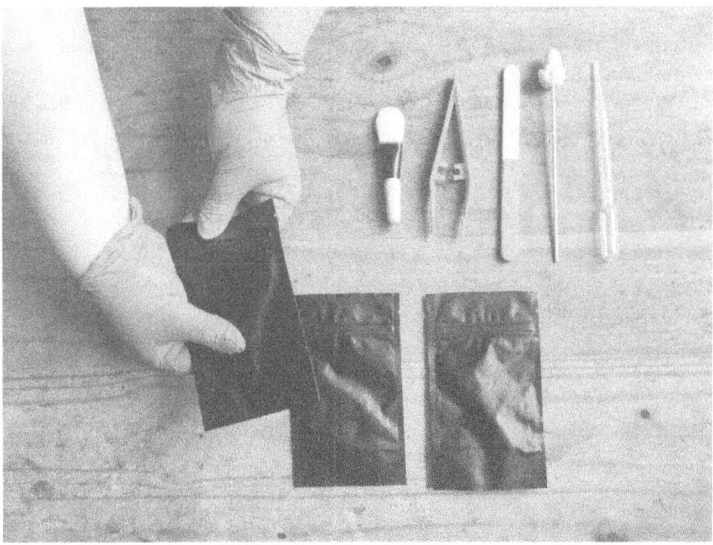

Figure 5.1 A picture of the materials featured in Guess-the-tool bag activity from *Haf o Hwyl* (Summer of Fun).

Photo by Morgan Fox.

Vacuuming a Teddy Bear

A multisensory activity (with sound as well as touch) where we had dusted some of my teddy bears with faux dust (potato flour, a highly visual but low-allergen and low-cost simulant), and children were invited to use brushes and a Museum Vac® to remove the dust.

Cleaning Muddy Tiles Swab Station

A multistage activity station where kids could roll their own cotton swab (or use store-bought ones) for mud removal from a small tile using small amounts of water. I had gathered the tiles from a local showroom for free and dipped them in mud together with my intern in the run-up to the event.

Paper Cleaning

An activity station where children could use small sponges and brushes to remove dust and soot from pieces of paper. This station was headed up by our paper conservator who had plenty of supplies to spare.

Hinging Artwork in Pre-Cut Mounts

An activity station where kids could frame a pretty piece of paper or an illustration from a book in a pre-cut mount using acid-free tape. They could then take it home and have it framed as a keepsake. Again, this station was headed up by my paper conservator colleague who had ample supplies.

Coloring Illustrations and Solving Conservation Jigsaw Puzzles

An unmanned station with activity sheets (coloring-in and spot-the-difference sheets I had illustrated and printed off), colored pencils, and two conservation jigsaw puzzles. The puzzles were printed illustrations of Greek urns pasted onto black foam board from another project and cut into pieces to mimic a broken ceramic.

Meeting the Materials

A largely unmanned activity station where materials could be explored via touch and sight. This included samples of leather or paper for touching and handling. A digital microscope was also set up over a scrap of leather, so participants could see a close-up of the grain on an adjacent screen.

Each activity could be done with both older and younger children and included elements of play, questioning, creativity, and fine-motor skills. There were a variety of textures, tools, and levels of messiness that felt inclusive toward neurodiversity and various comfort levels.

Drawing on my experience working with museum educators, I created a lesson plan with a description of each station, its materials, and key discussion points that could be scaled up or down depending on the age and ability of the children. For example, at the pottery station, we might engage young children about how and why things break and why we fix them. With older kids, we may go into more detail about what happens if we don't have all the pieces, when and why we gap-fill, or why our glues might take a long time to dry.

Talking to young audiences about conservation is one of the most fun things I can think of! With our early learners we found that turning things into a game (how fast can you roll a swab?), leaving room for improvised storytelling, or encouraging problem-solving (what would you do if your teddy got dusty?) worked best. Most of all, we loved asking and answering questions!

Feedback and Future Activities

Throughout the day, program staff did their best to ask participants what they enjoyed about the event and what could have been better, as much as possible when surrounded by lots of activity, giggling, and questions from our intended audience. Front-of-house staff at the museum asked similar questions of people on their way out of the venue and kept track of numbers and a rough estimate of the ages of the participants. No formal evaluation, like a survey, was collected at the event.

Overall people were delighted. Caregivers told me they were pleasantly surprised to learn about the profession and children ranged from politely interested to wildly enthusiastic. The other facilitators reported similar sentiments. Parents and guardians broadly expressed that they stumbled upon the activity day and thought better advertising would have bolstered numbers. The youngest children were most enamored by the tactile experiences around rolling swabs, guessing tools, and putting something broken back together again. This took on an amusingly competitive edge as siblings competed against one another in speed-assembling broken pots for much of the day!

Would I do anything differently? Definitely. Next time I would love for the meet-and-greet station to be more visually interesting, as it took coaxing to get people engaged in a way that was not true for the other activity tables. I found that bringing photographs of conservators doing things just did not capture the attention of anyone under the age of adulthood but drawings and illustrations worked well. On a mundane level, I would bring bins and separate recycling, especially for gloves, as these were requested by the children and a wonderful reminder that the next generation are passionate about preserving the planet. I would also have had a social media hashtag for the event so that caregivers could share photos and more easily discover group photographs afterwards.

I think the most important lessons learned were that kids can truly make anything into a game, caregivers love getting involved alongside their little ones, and conservators can have fantastic conversations with even the youngest minds. Oh, and children of all ages are obsessed with free pencils or any giveaway really. Even really dull ones!

Acknowledgments

I sincerely thank Carmarthenshire Museum Service (CofGâr), the Welsh government, and the Federation of Museums and Art Galleries of Wales for the funding that made the "Summer of Fun: Kids in Conservation" event possible. It was an absolute hoot, and my hope is that we can do it again!

None of this would have been possible without my team of brilliant conservation communicators: besides myself, the outreach facilitators included paper conservator Philippa Räder ACR, conservation students Leonie McKenzie and Emma Thomas, and the museum's in-house conservator Jo Cook ACR. On a practical level, we were all familiar with each other's activity stations, so we could swap or provide lunch and breaks, especially as some of us had chronic pain and needed to sit down or retreat regularly; their ability to task switch and adapt to each group in front of them was invaluable.

Biography

Jenny Mathiasson is an objects conservator in private practice in Wales, United Kingdom. Jenny studied conservation at Cardiff University in the United Kingdom before doing a Heritage Learning course with Linnaeus University in Sweden. Part of her work for the past ten years has included outreach activities with people of all ages and abilities, ranging from touch tours with the elderly to STEAM activity days for kids. She is also the co-founder, executive producer, and voice of *The C Word: The Conservators' Podcast*.

6 Little Conservators

Transforming a Pilot into a Recurring Program

Kathleen Lau

Introduction

More than thirty years ago, the Singapore government set out to map the first blueprint for the city-state's arts and culture landscape.[1] Since then, the impact of the policies has established cultural vibrancy in Singapore's art institutions and museums, cherished national icons and household names. The first of two strategic directions of the current version of the cultural masterplan states the goal of "[b]ringing arts and culture to everyone, everywhere, every day" and aims to reach new audiences, such as youth, to nurture the next generations of arts and culture participants.[2] Therefore, in 2018, the Ministry of Education implemented the Art Syllabus, a core but non-examinable subject for primary and lower secondary school students aged seven to fourteen. Exposing children to art in the first year of formal school provides an avenue to learn about themselves, the world around them, and better prepare them for future challenges and opportunities in the twenty-first century. Students are exposed to drawing, museum-based learning, and exhibitions as part of everyday curriculum in an expanded effort to sustain lifelong engagement.[3]

The National Heritage Board (NHB) is a statutory board under the Ministry of Culture, Community and Youth (MCCY), formed in 1993; its role is to safeguard and promote the heritage of Singapore's diverse communities for the purpose of education, nation-building, and cultural understanding. The Heritage Conservation Centre (HCC) is the repository and conservation facility for the management and preservation of Singapore's National Collection and supports the collections and exhibitions of eleven national and visual arts museums. Up until a few years ago, its outreach initiatives and programs were geared toward adults working in the industry, interested docents or the museum-going public. The HCC organizes facility tours and conducts talks on collections care and the National Collection.

DOI: 10.4324/9781003333210-8

Program Creation and Evolution

Outreach to younger audiences is a very recent development for HCC, and the origins of the "Little Conservators" program were born out of a serendipitous request in 2018. The NHB Staff Recreation Committee was looking for volunteers to be involved in a complementary program with the aim of helping young audiences distinguish between the roles of conservator and curator. Little Conservators was to follow Little Curators, a program that was part of "Bring Your Kids to Work Day."

Textiles Conservators Vanessa Liew and Siti Suhailah, Objects Conservator Sylvia Haliman, and Paintings Conservator Roger Lee volunteered their time for the program, sharing their passion for conservation and expressing their creativity in new ways. This was their first time engaging with children as part of an outreach program. Since this was an in-person event and happened after the Little Curators segment (conducted in the museum galleries), the conservators wanted to focus on conservation activities associated with being onsite at museums, which is predominantly about preventive aspects of conservation. This was presented in a more relatable way to the children by educating them on the dos and don'ts in a museum, such as why eating is not allowed or why the museum is always dark.

The program started with an introduction to the profession, then continued with show-and-tell about preventive conservation, which covered the agents of deterioration. The team felt that pests would be an exciting topic to emphasize why eating or drinking is not allowed in galleries. Children have a natural inclination toward creatures, and the team deliberately chose silver fish, termites, and clothes moths to represent the very common types of museum pests found in the collections. A pest rhyme was composed as a way of introducing and describing the physical appearance and the favorite "food" of the pests. For the activity "hide-and-seek" segment, the room was set up with different props, such as paintings, textiles on mannequins, piles of books, and furniture, for the children to either adopt the role of the pest and hide behind object props or grab different pest cutouts and place them on object prop. The program objective was to promote learning through fun, which was evident through the children's active participation and many questions throughout. The children, who were accompanied by their parents, participated actively and asked many interesting questions. The cozy group size of fifteen children and adults combined allowed for lively interaction between the four conservators and participants, all of whom thoroughly enjoyed the experience.

The 2018 program was meant to be a one-off; however, the COVID-19 pandemic brought about an unexpected development leading to the revival of the Little Conservators program. During the peak of the pandemic, where public social gatherings were banned and museum visitorship ground to a halt in Singapore, the Education and Community Outreach (ECO) department, a division under NHB that promotes the awareness of and engagement with heritage among Singaporeans, organized a "community of practice" forum as a platform for the regular sharing of outreach activities across NHB institutions as a way of enabling pan-institution collaboration and facilitating communities of practice to foster excellence. Sylvia shared her 2018 experience with the forum and was met with great enthusiasm from the ECO colleagues. HCC thus collaborated with ECO to revive Little Conservators as a pilot program under HeritageCares, an NHB initiative that reaches out to underserved communities in Singapore.

Reviving Little Conservators

The original team members were approached to be involved in the planning and conducting of a new version while still retaining the original program title. The team wanted to showcase the traits, skills, and attitudes that a conservator should possess. This led to the program being centered around hands-on activities in the hope that it would foster a love of working with their hands. The conservators wished to impart traits and attitudes such as patience, attention to detail, and curiosity, as well as having a slow and steady hand. As with the first event, the motivation was to make it fun and playful for children to understand more about the profession in a simple yet insightful manner.

The program starts with an introduction to the profession, distilled into three relatable roles that conservators play in their line of work: doctor, historian, and detective. This is done with the help of a larger-than-life artifact "friend" named "Roger the Radio," a 1950s wooden radio that was conserved by one of the team members and currently on display at the National Museum of Singapore. "Roger the Radio," who is dusty and infested with pests, is crying out for help! (Figure 6.1)

The first practical activity teaches basic surface cleaning using a cotton wool-rolled swab moistened with water on an artificially dusty wooden object, livened up by a cleaning song to the tune of "Hokey Pokey," which incorporates instructions on how to roll and swab.

> **Roll-ey swab-ey song**
> *1st verse*
> *You take your satay stick up*
> *You take your cotton wool out*
> *And you poke it all about*
> *You do the rolly rolly and it turns itself around...*
> *That's what it's all about!*
> *2nd verse*
> *You place your dry cotton swab into the water container*
> *You take your cotton swab out*
> *And you roll it all about...on the object!*
> *You do the swabbing, swabbing and it cleans all around....*
> *That's what it's all about!*

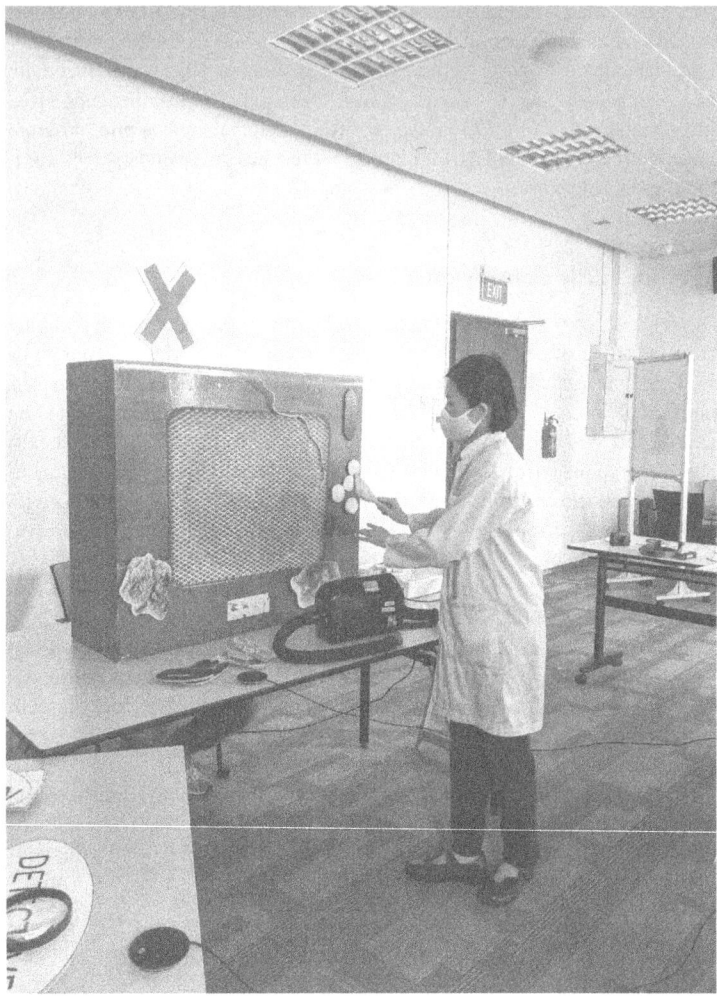

Figure 6.1 Sylvia demonstrating on "Roger the Radio."

Image courtesy of the Heritage Conservation Centre, National Heritage Board, Singapore.

The second practical activity introduces an essential painting conservation skill: color-matching and in-painting losses (or retouching). The activity is simplified to use basic colors to color-match the missing paint area on a printed image of an artwork by using either dots or lines in order to introduce the *Tratteggio* conservation technique.

The team presents the activities in the manner of a children's variety show, where various experts come to present different segments. This was live-streamed to the children at a student care center on the other end of the island. Student care centers provide before- and after-school care for school-going children (seven to fourteen years), who have no alternative childcare arrangements at home after the school day ends.

General programs, such as talks conducted by NHB or by HCC, are all conducted in English. Singapore has four official and equal languages (English, Chinese, Malay, and Tamil). However, the lingua franca between Singaporeans is English, and this is also the main medium of instruction in schools and at work. Conservators are aware that they often use technical jargon, so for the program, the team simplified the words and spelled out difficult terms to make the content age-appropriate. Music was also incorporated; the "Roll-ey Swab-ey" song created a lively, happy atmosphere while teaching the surface cleaning activity and catching the children's interest and attention.

Activity Kits Preparation

When choosing from the plethora of conservation techniques, consideration of health and safety was foremost, therefore no needles, scalpel blades, or solvents were included, and safety advice was communicated to the children while demonstrating the rolling of the cotton wool around the sharp applicator (satay) sticks. To keep costs low, the team used recycled materials and materials available in the labs. Funds were reserved for certain items, such as paint sets and papier mâché, and the team managed to keep expenses under 230 USD for thirty activity kits. The components of each activity kit needed to be portable and compact enough to be sent to the student care center before the actual event. The kits tested improvisational skills; for example, in making conservation dustbins out of small plastic containers, participants were given a real-life example of how used cotton swabs can be safely discarded. Regardless of the program platform, whether online or in-person, each child is given materials to carry out the activities (Figure 6.2). The objective is for them to bring the kit home to continue the activity, as it is not possible to complete the full treatment during the session.

The activities and materials were tested ahead of time. For the "in-painting" activity, it took several trials before settling on the artwork to be printed on A4 (US letter-sized) paper pasted on a board with missing paint areas. All mock-ups were also tested by the paintings conservator's eight-year-old daughter and evaluated for age-level suitability. Sustainability-wise, all the materials in the kit can be repurposed or recycled for other craft activities. The props and signages were also kept, as these could be reused for future programs.

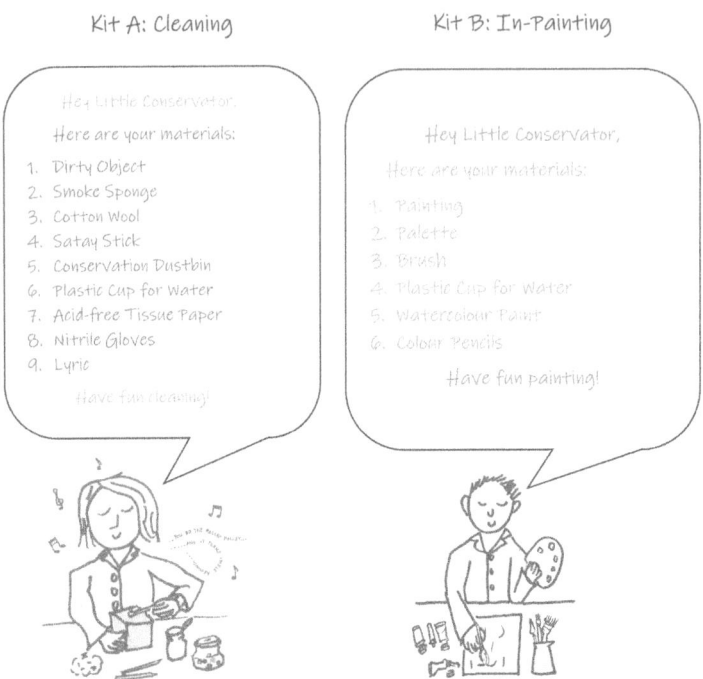

Kit A: Cleaning

Hey Little Conservator,

Here are your materials:

1. Dirty Object
2. Smoke Sponge
3. Cotton Wool
4. Satay Stick
5. Conservation Dustbin
6. Plastic Cup for Water
7. Acid-free Tissue Paper
8. Nitrile Gloves
9. Lyric

Have fun cleaning!

Kit B: In-Painting

Hey Little Conservator,

Here are your materials:

1. Painting
2. Palette
3. Brush
4. Plastic Cup for Water
5. Watercolour Paint
6. Colour Pencils

Have fun painting!

Figure 6.2 List of kit contents for cleaning and in-painting activities.

Image courtesy of the Heritage Conservation Centre, National Heritage Board, Singapore.

Challenges

The Little Conservators pilot program was conducted in December 2021. Singapore's COVID-19 measures then were gradually being lifted and expanded to allow for larger group gatherings; however, kids aged five to eleven were mostly unvaccinated as the vaccine had just been approved for use for this age group at the start of the month. Amidst very challenging and dynamic pandemic restrictions, the team had to drop the idea of an in-person event early on and execute an online program.

Conservators are known to be reserved by nature and like anyone new to performing, the team learned to embrace this element. Interacting with participants through a screen meant that there was a need to adopt a more theatrical style of presentation involving voice projection and big gestures so that the audience was kept engaged. The team also felt a written script was needed to help stay within the time set for the various scenes but left room for spontaneous ad-libs. Rehearsals helped with getting comfortable in front of the camera. Through practice and feedback from colleagues and the student care teachers, the team worked out the finer details of where to position themselves, lighting, voice projection, and tried with and without background music.

In terms of technology, the team had to quickly familiarize themselves with the ins and outs of using online platforms to stream the event to the kids at the student care center. Microsoft Teams was the only option as it was the only approved platform allowed for use with external parties, due to strict internet restrictions within the Singapore Public Service. The teleconferencing setup utilized microphones and video recording capabilities, so the participants could hear and follow instructions easily.

Working closely with partners but hampered by the physical barriers of non-contact was challenging. To ensure the event proceeded smoothly, the team met the student care center teachers online to brief them on the program outline and provide a set of instructions on some added preparatory steps when handling and distributing the activity kits to the children. The teachers at the student care center also played an important role in facilitating the activities on the ground, joining rehearsals to get comfortable with the program and becoming extensions of the conservators themselves who could not be there in person.

Another aspect that was not as straightforward was deciding which object from the National Collection would be appropriate and linked to the program activities, bearing in mind that the artifact should not be too complex, rare, nor ancient but rather something that is ordinary yet an important part of Singapore history. The "artifact friend" needed to be made larger-than-life for comical effect but also to be noticeable on screen. Role-playing dialogues, taking place between artifact and conservator, helped the children understand some of the ethics in the profession, such as knowing when to stop, how to respect an artifact, and how to foster a sense of responsibility toward an artifact.

Lessons Learned

Little Conservators is still in an early and experimental stage, and there is so much more room for further growth and exploration. The original team members created the content for both programs. For the online pilot, it was intended to lay the foundation by having a script and outline of the activities to enable future teams of conservators to take on and conduct the program using the same content. However, the content could be adapted to having a different hands-on activity or conservation skill or use a different "artifact friend." This allows other colleagues opportunities to participate offering unique synergies, depending on the composition of the team involved. For example, if a paper conservator is part of the team, the practical activity might feature a technique from paper conservation. If a conservation scientist is involved, the program can also evolve to showcase this specialty.

For a children's program, interaction in real life would have been more beneficial and enjoyable for both the participants and trainers, similar to the sentiments felt by ECO. The team loved children and felt it would be more meaningful to explore interactions between conservators and younger generations as they rarely come across children in their line of work. They also had to learn to slow down to match the children's pace of doing things. This was something learned at the actual event. Observing little details really emphasized the point of how different it is to work with children. Putting on gloves required a fair bit of time for small hands and rolling cotton swabs is fiddly and required more attempts to get the hang of it.

With each subsequent event, working with children enabled the original team members to develop greater sensibility and understand this target audience. The members also learned that children are curious by nature, happy to learn, and open to being taught how to do things. For example, at the in-person event, the team fondly recalled the unexpected and often funny responses and actions, the strong engagement, and surprise at how well the children absorbed the information. The online event only allowed the children to come up to the camera at the end of the program to provide feedback or their thanks.

Future Developments

With the opening of the new Children's Museum Singapore in late 2022, this new addition to the museum landscape demonstrates that children are an important audience. The next run of the Little Conservators will be held at this new venue in late 2023 on paintings and paper conservation with activities on in-painting and filling losses. On the national front, there is a stronger push and interest to involve younger audiences in the arts and heritage sector. The hope is to see more exhibitions tailored for children, more support, and greater interest of conservation-based outreach programs for this target group.

For the Little Conservators program itself, time spent for preparation should be reduced if resources allow. For example, the activity kits take up a significant amount of time to prepare and pack, and hopefully in time, this aspect can be handled solely by volunteers, thus freeing up precious time for conservation work. Volunteers and educators can also help in other aspects, such as program facilitation or guiding the children through the museum tour. The presentation of the program can also be improved with better equipment or digital platforms and ideally, an IT professional to handle the backend running and troubleshooting during the program. With more funding, certain segments of the program could be pre-recorded and directed by a professional producer. The program could potentially further its reach and tweaked to cater to kindergarten children and older teenagers.

Even though HCC is mainly a working institution performing a critical support role, as public officers and stewards of public resources in the Public Service, outreach is also a key area we must continue work on and is one of the ways we provide access to the National Collection.

Acknowledgments

Heartfelt gratitude to the HCC colleagues: Deputy Director (Conservation Services) Christel Pesme, Assistant Director (Management & Operations) Darren Wong, and my team members who created Little Conservators: Sylvia Haliman, Roger Lee, and Siti Suhailah, for the opportunity to write this article and your strong support. I'm deeply appreciative of all your time taken to provide valuable guidance, inputs, and feedback throughout the writing process. Without all your assistance, this chapter would not have been accomplished.

Biography

Kathleen Lau is a Senior Manager, and part of the Outreach and Capability Development team at the Heritage Conservation Centre (HCC), Singapore. Since 2016, she has managed the various outreach programs, including volunteers and media content, to increase awareness of HCC's role and unique support function of the working institution. Due to an increasing interest and need for collections care knowledge and practicum, the outlook in the coming years is to share HCC's expertise more extensively with schools, arts students, heritage enthusiasts/societies, and individuals.

Notes

1 Report of the Advisory Council on Culture and the Arts (ACCA 1989) is the signature document which laid the path for Singapore's arts development in the late 20th century. Arts and Culture Strategic Review (ACSR 2012) was initiated in 2010 to chart the next phase of cultural development in Singapore, all the way to 2025.

2 One of the two strategic directions from the Arts and Culture Strategic Review report (ACSR 2012).

3 ARTSYLLABUS Primary One to Six: Implementation starting with 2018 Primary One Cohort & ARTSYLLABUS Lower Secondary: Implementation starting with 2018 Secondary One Cohort (Ministry of Education 2018).

References

ACCA (Advisory Council on Culture and the Arts). 1989. *Report of the Advisory Council on Culture and the Arts*. Singapore: ACCA.

ACSR (Arts and Culture Strategic Review). 2012. *The Report of the Arts and Culture Strategic Review*. Singapore: ACSR. https://www.nac.gov.sg/docs/default-source/

resources-files/arts-masterplan/arts-and-culture-strategic-review-(2012)/the-report-of-the-arts-and-culture-strategic-review.pdf?sfvrsn=b64d33c4_2.

Ministry of Education, Singapore. 2018a. *ARTSYLLABUS Primary One to Six: Implementation Starting with 2018 Primary One Cohort.* Singapore: Student Development Curriculum Division. https://www.moe.gov.sg/-/media/files/primary/2018_primary_art_syllabus.pdf.

Ministry of Education, Singapore. 2018b. *ARTSYLLABUS Lower Secondary: Implementation Starting with 2018 Secondary One Cohort.* Singapore: Student Development Curriculum Division. https://www.moe.gov.sg/-/media/files/secondary/syllabuses/arts-ed/2018_lowersec_art_syllabus.pdf.

7 Persevering and Preserving after a Disaster

Introducing Youth to Glass Conservation

Claire Cuyaubère, Aimée Bou Rizk, and Amelia Youssef

Introduction

The American University of Beirut (AUB) Archaeological Museum is the third oldest museum in the Near East, after Cairo and Constantinople (now Istanbul), established in 1868. The AUB Archaeological Museum has around 21,000 objects in its collection covering Near-Eastern archaeology from the Early Stone Age to the Islamic Period, showcasing collections from seven countries: Lebanon, Syria, Cyprus, Palestine, Egypt, Iraq, and Iran. The collection includes a variety of material culture, from flint tools to pottery and glass vessels, terracotta and metal figurines, as well as Palmyrenean busts, marble sculptures, metal weapons, jewelry, and coins.

The museum does not have a conservation lab nor a conservator on staff. While Lebanon does not have a conservation training program on its territory, a cultural heritage preservation program was created in 2021 at the Lebanese University Fine Arts Academy (ALBA). The few formally trained conservators active in Lebanon were trained abroad.

On August 4, 2020, a massive explosion at the port of Beirut caused over 200 deaths, with numerous injured and displaced, and extensive material damage in the city. Located about two miles from the port, the museum's windows and doors were blown up, and a display case containing seventy-four archaeological glass vessels detached from its wall and toppled over. Of these vessels dating from the Roman, Byzantine, and Islamic periods, seventy-two shattered onto the gallery's marble floor, mixed-up with the glass from the showcases as well as from the shelves. Glass conservator Claire Cuyaubère traveled from France to Beirut, Lebanon, on an emergency mission followed by two conservation campaigns in 2021 and 2022 to lead the recovery of the fragments and reconstruction of the most complete vessels.[1] Claire's arrival provided an opportunity for conservation youth outreach at the museum.

DOI: 10.4324/9781003333210-9

American University of Beirut Educational Programming

The AUB Archaeological Museum has been organizing the "Children's Program" since 1980. They are usually held four times a year on Sunday morning, and each one of them focuses on a different theme inspired by the museum collection.

The Children's Program Officer, a volunteer committee member of the Society of the Friends of the Museum, prepares the activity with the help of the museum staff. Amelia Youssef has been the Children's Program Officer since 2019. Several volunteers from the local community also assist in the preparation of the activity and during the day of the program.

The general program is aimed for children aged between seven and thirteen. The museum has the capacity to host a maximum of eighty children per program, which was the usual number reached before the COVID-19 pandemic. Unlike a family program, the parents and caregivers drop the children off at the museum in the morning and pick them back at the end of the program around midday. The total duration of the program is usually around three and a half to four hours.

The program starts with a fifteen-to-thirty-minute presentation specifically prepared for the day with basic historic notions on the chosen topic. It is then followed by a targeted visit of the museum that gives context to the facts discussed. The children are engaged as much as possible during the presentation through questions and answers around the program theme. They are divided into two age groups (seven-to-ten-year-olds in one group and eleven-to-thirteen-year-olds in the other one) and by language, as the presentation is given in both English and French. This also helps adapt the program and activity to younger learners. Before beginning the next part of the program, the children gather outside the museum for a fifteen-minute snack break arranged by the museum, consisting of *man'ouche* (traditional Lebanese flatbread) and soft drinks.

The Study Collection Hall, a multipurpose room at the museum, is set out with tables of ten and all the supplies required for the hands-on activity part of the program. The tables are also divided by age to facilitate communication and distribution of materials. Each table is supervised by one volunteer or a museum staff member, two for tables of younger children; the adults explain the activity and help the children as necessary. About ten adults are usually present for each program. This section usually consists of an art activity with samples prepared ahead of time. The museum staff and the volunteers select the final methodology and materials after a series of trials. Several levels of difficulty are developed to appeal to the wide age range, with easier variants of the activities for the youngest and more challenging for the older ones. The activity length varies between an hour and a half and two hours, framed by breaks before and after this part of the program. No formal break is scheduled during the activity, but children are able to step away as they need, letting them refocus at their own rhythm.

Special programs are occasionally organized on technical themes where a specialist volunteers their time to give a presentation and help during the manual activity. In a special program held in 2016, titled "Restoring the Past," Beirut-born objects conservator, Natalie Hanna, gave a presentation on ceramics conservation with a hands-on demonstration before helping the children restore their own broken pots.

Glass Conservation Educational Program

In 2022, the AUB organized an international two-day conference titled "Through Shattered Glass," which coincided with the United Nations International Year of Glass. The multidisciplinary workshop addressed glass archaeology, glass conservation, and material science, among other topics. A youth program at the museum on the topic of glass was planned around that conference, and Claire's presence made it possible for a slightly different format with a focus on glass conservation.

Due to the focus of the program and the specificity of the hands-on activity, and in the global context of pandemic, the group was reduced to twenty to twenty-five children, aged six to twelve. Despite the initially suggested age range of eight to eleven, several kids slightly below or above that age range were accepted when they were coming with a sibling within the targeted age range. The presence of younger children influenced the choice of the hands-on activity and supplies. The children were divided by age range during the activity and the youngest were given cups broken into fewer fragments to make the first assembly easier for them.

One of the objectives of the program is to raise awareness of archaeology, cultural heritage, and local history. The museum team is also particularly interested in topics of preservation and conservation, its Director Dr. Nadine Panayot being a founding partner of the cultural heritage preservation training program at ALBA. Within the specific context of the 2020 Beirut port explosion, it felt especially important to organize a program around the theme of heritage destruction, reconstruction, preservation, and the conservation efforts stirred by the shattered glass collection at the museum. The museum staff, however, had not undertaken a conservation-themed program without the presence of a conservator. At the time of the conference, the museum staff and Amelia were planning the next Children's Program. The theme of glass was already in their minds, but Claire's presence at the AUB made the idea of a conservation-oriented program possible. Amelia took this opportunity to ask her if she would like to be part of the program, and Claire agreed to volunteer her time and expertise. Rather than create a new program, the team utilized the pre-existing format of the Children's Program.

Claire brought guidance not only to prepare the activity but also gave the glass conservation demonstration on the day of the program and helped supervise it, while Amelia and the museum staff took care of the logistics and the organization of the program.

Preparations

Although the theme of the program was glass, for obvious safety reasons, having children play with broken glass was not an option. Because the usual Children's Program programming does not focus on conservation, it was necessary to adapt the activity to accommodate locally available supplies. Hard, clear plastic stem cups (usually for serving wine or champagne) were chosen as an alternative.

Pre-program tests with Claire, the staff, and volunteers were necessary to determine how to best break the cups and which adhesive was suited for the assembly of plastic cup fragments by children. Due to budget limitations, cheaper and readily available supplies were preferred. Using a water-based adhesive was a strong criterion of choice for children aged as young as six. Program volunteers ensured they could break the plastic cups without warping them (thus making reconstruction possible) through trial and error.

Presentation

The first part of the program was given by Amelia and museum assistants. Aimée Bou Rizk, a trained archaeologist working at the museum since 2014, is a museum assistant with an active role in the program. They started by asking the children to brainstorm the various uses of glass in everyday life. Then, the historic presentation covered the invention of glass and that of Phoenician glassblowing in modern-day Lebanon, as well as later technological progress. This specificity of local history made it easy to illustrate the presentation with artifacts in the collection. How glass ages and degrades was also introduced in simple terms that were understandable to the youngest in the group (additional info was given to older children who asked more specific questions about archaeology and science). The impact of the 2020 Beirut port explosion on the museum's building and collection was also presented, including the emergency and conservation missions that followed.

Hands-on Activity

The hands-on activity took place in the museum galleries. It consisted of the reconstruction of hard plastic cups that had been previously broken by the program staff and individually bagged. Claire started with a demonstration on how to identify connecting fragments and do a dry reconstruction using

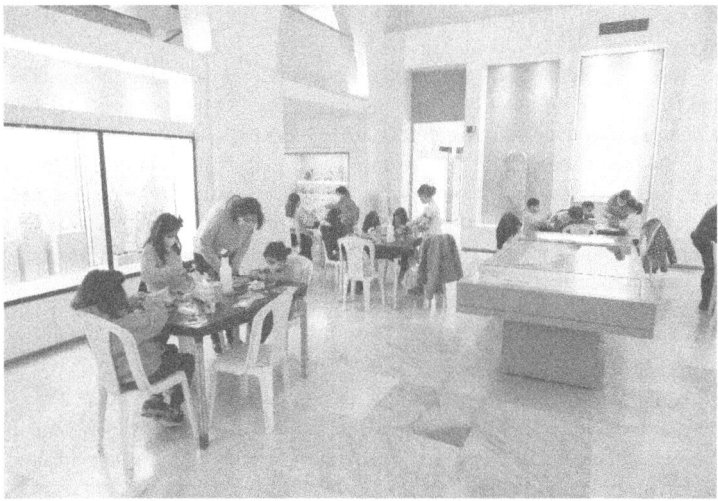

Figure 7.1 Children reconstructing plastic cups during the hands-on activity.
© The Archaeological Museum at the American University of Beirut, Lebanon.

masking tape to better understand how the fragments fit together and the preferred order of assembly. The demonstration continued with the use and application of the adhesive and how to maintain the fragments properly aligned using masking tape.

The children could then start their "conservation treatment" on their own cup. They were seated at tables of four. Each child was handed a couple broken cups in plastic bags and did the puzzle work and assembly at their own rhythm with the conservator, educators, and museum assistants navigating between tables and helping or giving directions and advice as needed. This allowed the adults to adapt their level of intervention to the age and abilities of each child. Younger children were given cups broken into fewer fragments (around four to five shards) while older ones assembled cups broken into about a dozen fragments and were handed additional cups as needed. The hands-on part of the program lasted for about ninety minutes to two hours (Figure 7.1).

Lessons Learned

The program was successful, and the team received good oral feedback both from children and caregivers. From the feedback, program organizers learned that the room where the demonstration took place got a little crowded when the children gathered around Claire, eager to see and to ask lots of questions.

An easy solution would be to divide the group during the demonstration and to repeat it.

While the majority of participants seemed to enjoy the activity and have fun, a few (not necessarily the younger participants) did not show a lot of patience in the hands-on part and tended to jump to the assembly of the fragments without doing dry reconstruction first, resulting in less satisfying joins and reconstruction. On the other hand, a twelve-year-old girl loved the experience so much that she was considering a career in conservation by the end of the program. The hands-on activity proved a bit difficult for the youngest children (around six years) and a little easy for the older ones (twelve years). It would be interesting to try a similar format with a smaller group that would also be more homogenous in age, which would allow program facilitators to better tailor the difficulty level.

Additionally, since the program was a one-time event (rather than a reoccurring one), it was necessary to implement a hands-on activity that could fit within a couple hours and be self-sufficient. A series of conservation-focused children's programs could allow for longer activities, as well as drying times. A take-home component would also be a way to make longer activities possible; this would, however, require an additional budget for the supplies to take home.

In general, the specificity of the glass conservation-related activity and the manual dexterity that it required calls for smaller and more age-homogenous groups, which would help cater better to the children's needs. This could make the hands-on part of the program more approachable to distinct age groups. It appears that conservation-themed programs could benefit from this slightly different format, compared to the usual one for The Children's Program. A possible variation could consist of mixing up fragments from several cups to increase the difficulty of the exercise for older children, while early learners would benefit from participating in a smaller group with a higher adult-to-child ratio.

From a conservator's point of view, putting together a children's program without having conservation supplies and equipment at hand required some additional adaptability, particularly in the choice of supplies for the program. They had to be found and bought within a few days from craft stores rather than specialized ones and during a time of shortages that Lebanon was facing at the time.

Overall, the pre-program preparation was an opportunity for museum assistants and program officer to practice reconstructing plastic cups and be able to better help the children during the hands-on activity. The demonstration was the added value and the most praised part of the program as shown by the reaction of the children and their endless stream of questions and enthusiasm during the explanations. Further training for the museum and program staff by a conservator could make it possible to reiterate such a program on a more regular basis.

Acknowledgments

The authors would like to thank the Society of the Friends of the AUB Archaeological Museum, who make the Children's Program possible through their continued support.

Biography

Claire Cuyaubère is a Ceramics, Glass and Enamel Conservator at the *Centre de Recherche et de Restauration des Musées de France* (C2RMF, French public museums' Conservation and scientific research center). After graduating from the *Institut National du Patrimoine* (INP, French National Institute for Cultural Heritage), she was an objects conservation fellow at the Smithsonian Institution's National Museum of Asian Art between 2012 and 2017. As a conservator in private practice then based in Paris, she led an emergency rescue mission in Beirut following the August 4, 2020, explosion, as well as two conservation campaigns in 2021 and 2022.

Aimée Bou Rizk is a Museum Assistant at the American University of Beirut's Archaeological Museum since 2014. She graduated in 2018 from the Lebanese University with a Master's degree in Art History and Archaeology, specializing in Hellenistic and Roman periods. She has several experiences in archaeological excavations in Lebanon since 2011. She is currently a PhD candidate at the Lebanese University.

Amelia Youssef was trained and worked as an archaeologist until 2000 but had a career shift and is now currently an instructor of English at the Lebanese American University. She has also been the Children's Program Officer at the American University of Beirut since 2018 where she conducts multiple activities related to children at the museum premises.

Note

1 The 2020 emergency mission as well as the following conservation campaign in 2021 were initiated and organized by the Institut National du Patrimoine (INP) in Paris and funded by the International Alliance for the Protection of Heritage in Conflict Areas (Aliph Foundation) in Geneva.

8 Art to Go

Sparking Wonder with the Littlest Learners

Sabine Kretzschmar and Colleen Snyder

Introduction

The Cleveland Museum of Art (CMA) is fortunate to have a robust Education Art Collection (EAC), which is comprised of about 10,000 cultural heritage objects from around the globe, spanning 5000 years. The EAC was started in 1914 to spread awareness of the visual arts and the newly opened CMA, founded in 1916. Savvy museum educators amassed global cultural collections to engage the art novice, such as paintings, works on paper, textiles, jewelry, sculpture, and functional objects, including design objects and exemplars of artistic processes. Works of art in this collection were organized into exhibitions of all sizes and lent free of charge to educational and civic organizations throughout Northeast Ohio. As the original intent was for exhibitions and not handling, the quality was relatively high compared to other educational collections. From 2000 to the present day, the collection has primarily been used in hands-on, facilitated programming at the CMA and in the community. This includes the "Art to Go" program where artworks are taken offsite to schools and other institutions. Each of these facilitated experiences has consistently demonstrated that audiences of all ages benefit immensely from direct access to works of art.

This case study highlights an Art to Go program for the littlest school learners, aged three to five years. Though these ages were represented in visitors that attended weekend family-focused programming, in-school programming had only been offered to primary school and older students. A neighboring preschool offered an opportunity for an in-classroom outreach experience, accelerated by the fact that a CMA conservator had a child enrolled there and could make introductions and inquiries. It is important to note that CMA has over a decade of successful collaboration between the Conservation and Education departments, including offering accessibility programming for blind or low-vision visitors, classroom programming for teens and young adults, and weekend family-focused events. The conservation outreach component of the Art to Go program was developed from existing programming for older students and then modified with adjusted language and expectations tailored to the preschool setting.

DOI: 10.4324/9781003333210-10

General Program Approach

The current Art to Go program is modeled on the object-based, hands-on learning approach that is fundamental to conservation practices. This practice of close looking and critical thinking explores the object's materials and history, including the use, wear, and repair that have contributed to the current appearance. This close looking naturally inspires discussion with peers to answer questions like "Who would have made or used this? What does the object remind you of in your own life? How did it get here?"

This programming is founded on a core principle that authentic objects "promote curiosity and critical engagement beyond that offered by replicas or digital recreations" (Bunce 2016). They generate more questions and form a vital part of the discussion. Their cracks, repairs, missing parts, and inscriptions are clues to their life; they are marks that witness their making and history. Each session is tailored to the age group: teenagers are supplied with more detailed worksheets, additional tools (such as magnifying glasses, measuring tapes, and flashlights), and they are asked to present their observations to the entire class. Kindergarten through second graders (aged five to eight) typically have abbreviated or no worksheets, use fewer tools, and require more educators to better supervise and lead discussions. Sessions for younger learners include more sensory-based activities, such as movement, sound, touch, or drawing, in order to enhance connection and the experience (Shaffer 2018).

Group size is a critical factor. When visiting schools, it can be difficult to mandate group sizes, though our ideal maximum is twenty students per suitcase of approximately six to ten art objects. Ideally, we aim for no more than five children per educator; however, we have successfully worked with groups as large as ten. CMA policy dictates that at least two staff members must travel with suitcases; though, with such labor-intensive programming, and the need to mitigate risk to objects during student handling, trained docents assist staff when possible. Educators set the tone, manage classroom conduct, create connections, spark wonder, and make the material relevant. As such, educational strategies, sourced from classroom teachers, museum educators, or youth leaders are incorporated into every program.

Young Learner Program Structure

In preparation for an Art to Go visit, we learn as much as possible about the students, classroom, and learning goals to find potential points of connection. Logistics are worked out to ensure an appropriate setup that will support the program's format and ensure the safety of the objects. They include the size, number, length of each class, and room setup. For example, we require a table for staging or several smaller tables for multiple groups of students, all clean and cleared with no food or beverages. We also ask that all students wash their hands before we arrive.

We start the session by introducing ourselves, the museum, and its collection, followed by a quick discussion on the safe handling of objects. It is especially helpful if students wear nametags so presenters can call on them by name. The first object is always chosen to be large enough so that we can have a discussion with the entire group, which serves as a good icebreaker and puts students in the mindset to engage with other artworks more deeply.

We invite participants to look without any explanation of the objects using modified Visual Thinking Strategies (VTS). Pioneered over thirty years ago by cognitive psychologist Abigail Housen and museum educator Philip Yenawine, VTS is a research-based pedagogy widely adopted by schools and museums for audiences of all ages that prioritizes student-centered, facilitated discussion as a way to encourage inclusive discussions and student-driven learning (Yenawine 2013). After the students make observations, we use prompts inspired by the object or employ other critical-thinking methodologies, including Harvard University's Project Zero's Thinking Routines Toolkit.[1]

We then break into smaller groups of three to four students. We set up three or more stations, each with an object and an educator. Educators facilitate student-led discussions with each group by asking them what they see, using open-ended questions and then allowing time for them to lead the discussion. We try to include a "mind-blowing" fact, something that they would not know from looking but sparks interest. This might be something like noticing the blue color of Chinese hair ornaments or a surprising material choice like cut kingfisher feathers. The age of an object is also often a point of fascination. They are encouraged to make connections between the object and their own lives through additional prompt questions: "What do you think this was used for? How was someone able to make this? What material(s) do you think created this?" as well as specifically conservation-focused questions, such as "How might these objects have arrived in their current condition? How might you preserve them for the next generation?" If time allows, we rotate the small groups, so they each have an opportunity to visit each station. At the end of the program, with the entire group, we invite them to reflect on the experience.

Choosing Objects and Considerations of Safe Object Handling

As with all aspects of this programming, choosing objects involves discussions between conservators and educators, balancing the need for an engaging variety of materials with the safety of the artworks. Objects must be relatively stable and of a size and weight that is easy to transport and handle. Artworks can be broken but should be without sharp edges or hazardous materials. Objects that have pesticides or other hazardous materials present are labeled and reserved for select uses where they can only be handled by trained, gloved staff.

For our youngest students, we select objects that have robust surfaces for handling, like glazed ceramics and cast bronzes. Metals may receive a proactive protective coating of sacrificial wax, much like many outdoor sculptures, and more fragile materials, like textiles or paper, will be mounted or framed before outreach.

Room setup is paramount to optimize direct observations and prevent breakage. Objects are always handled on open, clean tables or while sitting directly on the floor and placed in acid-free blueboard trays with additional foam or tissue padding to prevent rolling and evenly support the artworks. Students handle the objects only long enough to physically experience the texture and weight, view the underside or inside, or explore other important tactile features.

Considerations and Modifications for Youngest Learners

An opportunity arose to pilot a program specifically for early learners at a neighboring preschool called The Music Settlement. Founded only a few years before CMA, in 1912, it was designed to offer free or low-cost musical training to Cleveland's new immigrant population, and its mission is very similar to the museum's: to "learn, create, inspire and heal" through art and music. The preschool, founded in the 1950s, seeks to offer opportunities to children of all backgrounds, as part of a universal pre-K initiative in the county. Though the preschool had connections with CMA in previous years, staff changes, and the pandemic disrupted these ties. Recently, however, there was an opportunity to rebuild the relationship. We met with their early childhood director to work out content and logistics and together decided that sitting on the floor might be the best option for early learners in observing the artwork. Blueboard trays would help safeguard the objects as per the usual structure.

The objects themselves were chosen specifically for their engaging colors, materials, and textures, though it became immediately evident that they also had a relatable theme of animals. All handleable objects were ceramics or sturdy cast metals; all were small enough to be passed to little hands; and all had similarities and differences that could be used as jumping-off points for discussion. A large felt artwork would be used as the opening group discussion and held only by CMA staff (Figure 8.1).

The session began with the entire group in front of this artwork, which was most easily visible by an entire classroom and arguably the most colorful and engaging, allowing the kids to interact with CMA staff and priming them to engage in smaller groups later on. All eyes and ears were engaged for most of the programs, and the excitement was contagious. In fact, the main issue was getting children to speak in turns, as many shouted out

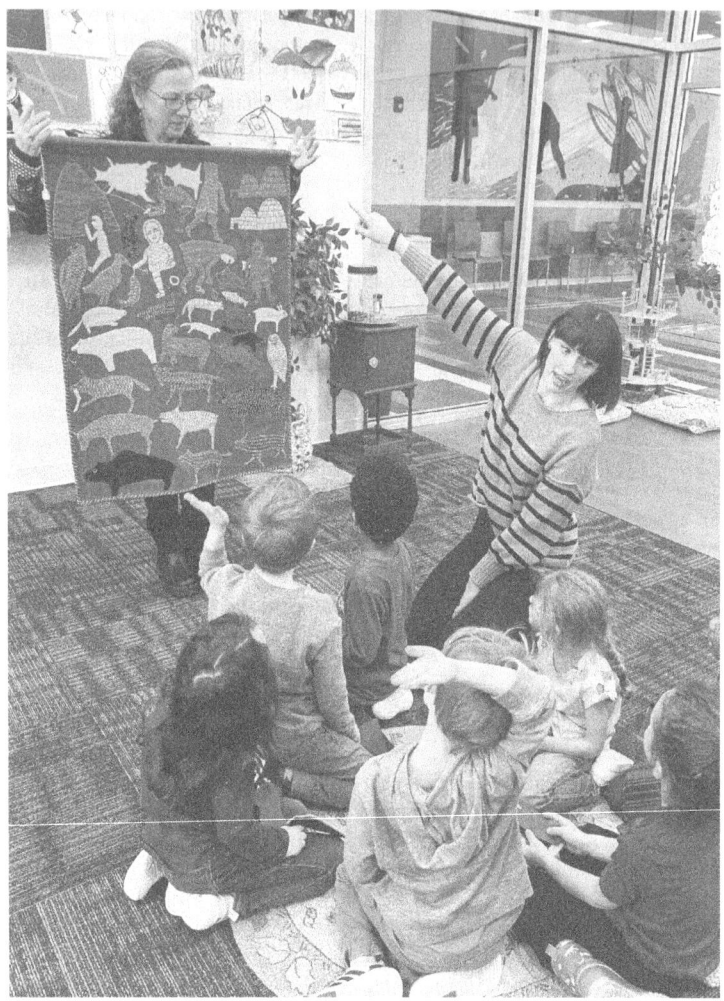

Figure 8.1 Opening discussion with the full group of students.

Image courtesy of Cleveland Museum of Art; photo by Colleen Snyder.

thoughts all at once, so a future consideration is skill-building for redirecting when the large conversation veers off topic. We handed the participants small felt squares, so they could get an idea of what the textile felt like, match colors, and keep bodies busy while talking and looking. The children were then invited to break up into small groups of three or four with the help of their teachers.

Each group spent a few minutes with a CMA facilitator and two objects in a tray. We began with a variant of the following: "Hello, friends! Let's all sit criss-cross, applesauce in front of this tray. We're going to start by looking with only our eyes (points to eyes) before we explore some more. What do you see in front of you?"

Once some initial thoughts were shared, we would offer a surprising fact: "Did you know that these objects are actually 100 years old?! They've been around longer than you or me, and we want them to be there 100 years from now, so I'll share with you how we can hold them carefully to explore a bit more." Students were invited one-at-a-time, through careful, two-handed passing of artworks over the tray, to feel the artworks and comment on size, weight, texture, and so forth. Rather than giving handling instructions at the outset, or talking about preservation directly, it was modeled as part of the exercise. One effective way of allowing touch while limiting risk included comparing the animal figures to pets the children might have at home. We explained how we "pet" the sculptures as carefully as we pet our own animals and using one or two light fingers was best. In fact, using a light touch in outreach exercises was borrowed from an observation by a visitor during a low vision tour: light fingers can feel the surface much better and mitigate chances of damage.

Just as with older learners, early learners intuitively understand materials based on their everyday interactions with the world. They were prompted the same way as the older students who work on conservation examination worksheets: what do you think this is made from? Hard or cold observations were equated with stone or metal fairly accurately, and comparisons of which was heavier or larger gave the opportunity to examine, think, and talk about what the object might be made from and what the artist intended it to represent. As with all sessions, it was very important that it be student-led, even if that meant the tiger was interpreted as a dinosaur (green and bumpy) or they shared a story of their own pet that had recently passed away. Once the students cycled through all four stations, the objects were quickly put back in the case, and we wished our new friends well and thanked them for sharing this time with us.

Feedback

At the conclusion of our visits, we solicited informal feedback from the director and teachers. The Music Settlement educators felt activities were age-appropriate, with the most popular object being the vibrantly colored felt mural panel. The school noted that kindergarten-aged students (aged five to six) were especially curious to know more about the geography and cultures of the people who created the artworks. Since the discussion was student-led, some of this information was relayed as it naturally fit into conversations, like how the artist lived in a northern climate with igloos depicted in felt cutouts. They requested photos of the artworks be shared afterward to post in the room for discussion points or further inspiration. One teacher requested that sessions be extended with an art-making option, like instructions for creating a collaborative felt collage inspired by the students' surroundings and experiences.

Though teachers reported that some groups felt rushed, the constructed time allotment had been carefully chosen because it has worked well with similarly aged children in the past. However, in the future, we could have a designated timekeeper, as some activities and transitions did get off schedule. As time allowed, additional conservation discussion was squeezed in: "Did you know that the careful way you are touching the object is just what I do at my job as a conservator? Conservators are people who help preserve artworks, so they last a long time, so your grandchildren can do this someday, too!" The Music Settlement has expressed interest in a follow-up program with more in-depth conservation content.

Lessons Learned

Overall, the structure was a successful adaptation of the Art to Go program for early learners. Gathering at the beginning to share the experience of taking in one larger artwork enabled the type of student-led discussion that primed them for experiencing the materiality of a smaller artwork that could be directly handled.

The selection of materials naturally lent itself to talking about animals. The relatability of animals and relatively recognizable creatures made for easy conversation between students and facilitators. As this was a pilot program, and there was a desire to test out the reception of activities with younger students, a few pre-session steps that are typically employed in the Art to Go program were set aside. These include sharing the artwork theme with teachers ahead of time, providing a Google Drive of images and object information, and handing out nametags for students and teachers. It is clear from school feedback that future sessions would benefit from these protocols.

It helped immensely to have one member who had expertise in early education to model both spoken language and body language. The words and actions chosen with students aged three to five are especially important and must echo the language they are accustomed to in order to retain attention and control over the activities. If no staff member with this specialty is available in the future, a discussion with teachers beforehand would be essential (or even ask if the teachers would be willing to handle this type of facilitation during the session).

We all readily agreed on the importance of re-establishing connections with a neighboring school that had a similar mission of outreach to the Cleveland community, and the students really seemed to benefit from the activities and interactions. To continue this pilot, we will need to look at the sustainability by lessening the time preparation, time away from the museum, and number of program facilitators. In the meantime, preschools will be encouraged to bring students to the museum for conservation-focused programming.

Learners of all ages really seem to benefit from direct contact with historic artifacts or objects, so an alternative could be to use a variety of non-collection items, such as those obtained at yard sales or vintage shops. Items that are broken or worn would serve to add interest and enliven conversations about the history of use. As conservator Chris Caple wrote in his 2006 book, objects can be considered as "reluctant witnesses to the past," and their meaning often needs to be extracted through close looking (Caple 2006). Materiality is the students' gateway to these experiences.

Student questions in sessions of all ages often involve conservation-related issues of materiality and degradation, and close collaboration between conservators and educators successfully lets students explore in a way to provide their own answers or produce answers with little direction. Once the program has been set and a few sessions have been run to work the kinks out, the initial time investment will pay off, and it can be repeated with comparatively less effort. After all, one of the best parts of working with the smallest learners is being confident enough in the material and lesson to appreciate the quirky comments and funny observations that three-to-five-year-olds can offer; you may just hear something like, "Wow, that sculpture is as old as my mom!"

Acknowledgments

The authors are indebted to the following individuals for helping to make a successful program in no particular order: Molly Phillips and Diana Rafferty for their excellent help planning and carrying out the pilot programs, Beth Edelstein for playing an important role in moving CMA/Education collaborations forward and incorporating additional outreach ideas and programs, Sarah Scaturro for supporting outreach endeavors, and Karen Heitlinger and colleagues for partnering with CMA staff and allowing us to pilot this program.

Biography

Colleen Snyder joined the Cleveland Museum of Art in 2010 as part of the building expansion project, where she continues to care for the encyclopedic collection, mentor students, and help develop outreach programming. As part of AIC's Education Outreach (K-12) Outreach Subcommittee, Colleen enjoys opportunities to present STEAM activities to kids and teachers. She is a 2008 graduate of the SUNY Buffalo State University Garman Art Conservation Program where she majored in the care of 3D objects with a minor in archaeological materials. Her current research focuses on CMA's ancient bronze statue of Apollo Sauroktonos, elucidating how it was cast and its original intended appearance.

Sabine Kretzschmar is the Manager of the Education Art Collection at the Cleveland Museum of Art. Kretzschmar earned her MA in Art History and Museum Studies from Case Western Reserve University, after majoring in Art History at the University of Wisconsin-Madison. Prior to her current role, she has worked as a curator, educator, and executive director for organizations including the University of Akron, the Akron Art Museum, and the Shaker Historical Society and Museum.

Note

1 For an excellent resource with a large selection of updated thinking routines see Harvard University's Project Zero website (Harvard University, Graduate School of Education 2022).

References

Bunce, Louise. 2016. "Appreciation of Authenticity Promotes Curiosity: Implications for Object-Based Learning in Museums." *Journal of Museum Education* 41, no. 3 (September): 230–39. https://doi.org/10.1080/10598650.2016.1193312.

Caple, Chris. 2006. *Objects: Reluctant Witnesses to the Past.* London: Routledge. https://doi.org/10.4324/9780203409060.

Harvard University, Graduate School of Education. 2022. "Project Zero's Thinking Routine Toolbox." Accessed 23 June, 2023. https://pz.harvard.edu/thinking-routines.

Shaffer, Sharon E. 2018. *Object Lessons and Early Learning.* New York, NY: Routledge. https://doi.org/10.4324/9780203702253.

Yenawine, Philip. 2013. *Visual Thinking Strategies: Using Art to Deepen Thinking Across School Disciplines.* Cambridge, MA: Harvard Education Press.

9 Art Matters Club

Integrating Conservation Outreach into After-School Curricula

Raquel Santos

Introduction

The International Baccalaureate Organization (IBO), commonly known as the IB, is a renowned institution that offers four high-quality educational programs. These programs are specifically designed to cater to a global network of schools with the shared objective of fostering a better and more harmonious world (IBO 2018). The IB's vision is to develop inquiring, knowledgeable, and caring young individuals who actively contribute to the creation of a more peaceful world through intercultural understanding and respect. In pursuit of this vision, the organization collaborates with schools, governments, and international organizations to create rigorous programs of international education. These programs aim to challenge students to become active, compassionate, and lifelong learners who recognize the value of diversity and appreciate that multiple perspectives can be valid.

Central to this approach is the acknowledgment and cultivation of the diverse capacities of students, including their physical, social, intellectual, aesthetic, and cultural dimensions. This commitment is deeply ingrained in the implementation of the Primary Years Programme (PYP), a comprehensive educational framework that embraces a transdisciplinary approach.

Catering to children aged three to twelve years, the PYP offers an inquiry-based framework that places the student at the center of their educational journey while nurturing conceptual understanding (IBO n.d.). Within this framework, IB schools seamlessly integrate museum and exhibition experiences into the PYP art curriculum, providing a platform that goes beyond academic development and fosters students' holistic growth. The PYP's dedication to recognizing and cultivating the diverse capacities of students aligns harmoniously with the immersive and interactive nature of museum learning.

However, the value of museums as sources of learning has become even more evident in light of the COVID-19 pandemic, which has highlighted the need for alternative approaches to object-based learning in the absence of in-person experiences. As a response to this challenge, digital technologies and virtual platforms have gained significant popularity, providing access

DOI: 10.4324/9781003333210-11

to cultural heritage, object-based learning, and education on conservation practices. Integrating these technologies into classrooms or school settings enhances the learning experience, overcoming the limitations of physical museums and exhibitions. This integration allows educators to offer students a captivating way to explore cultural heritage while promoting conservation practices.

The "Art Matters Club," a pilot after-school program for art conservation outreach, demonstrates this approach by aiming to integrate cultural heritage conservation into the PYP at the Gjøvikregionen International School, Gjøvik, Norway. By incorporating museum experiences and fostering exploration, the Art Matters Club initiative for PYP exemplifies how IB schools can create inclusive and comprehensive educational environments that embrace students' diverse capacities, promoting their overall development. Through this initiative, students actively engage with cultural heritage, develop critical thinking skills, foster creativity, and gain a deeper understanding of the world beyond the classroom. This integration not only enhances academic learning but also instills core values such as empathy, respect, and open-mindedness. Within the inquiry-based, transdisciplinary context of the PYP, students develop conceptual understanding and a sense of ownership in their educational journey. By investigating the practical implementation of the Art Matters Club at this school, this chapter provides valuable insights into the broader implications and potential benefits of integrating similar initiatives within the IB program, as well as other school and educational systems.

Background: Piloting Art Matters Club at Gjøvikregionen International School

Gjøvikregionen International School (GIS) is an international school that opened its doors in August 2015 in Gjøvik, Norway. Since its inception, the school has experienced remarkable growth, expanding from thirty students in 2015 to over 180 students in 2023. The increasing demand for enrollment has resulted in waiting lists across multiple grade levels. As an authorized IB World School, GIS offers both the "Primary Years Programme" and the "Middle Years Programme," empowering students with a well-rounded education. Our vision centers around diversity-powered and innovative learning, preparing students for their future educational pursuits, whether in the "IB Diploma Programme" or any other school of their choice worldwide.

At GIS, students benefit from a comprehensive curriculum that encompasses various disciplines, including music and art classes. Furthermore, our school provides a rich assortment of after-school activities, with offerings that change each semester. These extracurricular programs cater to a wide range of interests, including sports teams, language clubs, science and technology initiatives, and more. By consistently introducing new opportunities, students can continually explore their passions and discover new interests beyond the traditional classroom setting.

Aligned with GIS's mission to cultivate skilled and responsible global citizens deeply connected to their local community, the pilot Art Matters Club was a fitting extracurricular option during the fall semester of 2022. Inspired by the Smithsonian Institution's "Art and Me" family program, the club not only provided a unique and invaluable platform for students to engage in art conservation related activities but also fostered a deeper appreciation for the importance of preserving cultural heritage. Through this experience, students were encouraged to explore their own cultural backgrounds and pose thought-provoking questions, particularly within the context of an international school in Norway, a country that embraces people from diverse cultures. The Art Matters Club perfectly aligns with the school's mission to integrate art conservation into the IB curriculum and to raise awareness among young learners about the significance of safeguarding cultural heritage for future generations. It seeks to nurture global citizenship and instill a sense of responsibility in preserving our cultural resources.

Art Matters Club Program

The Art Matters Club program was specifically designed for 1st and 2nd grade students, aged six to eight, and served as an engaging extracurricular activity held in the school's art room throughout a semester. Considering the importance of individual attention and support, the club had a maximum limit of four participants. This limitation ensured that each student received the necessary guidance and assistance from the instructor during the sessions. Each session was planned, taking into account the students' ages and abilities. Prior to the sessions, trials and experiments were conducted to determine the most suitable methodology and materials for the activities, ensuring an age-appropriate and enriching learning experience.

The program commenced in September 2022 with a group of three students, aged five to seven, and continued with weekly forty-five-minute sessions that covered a wide range of art conservation topics. Throughout the series of nine sessions, the same group of students remained engaged and actively participated in the program. The selection of topics for each session was carefully based on three primary criteria: art medium/technique, seasonal celebrations in the school calendar, and weather and light conditions influenced by the unique geographical location of Norway. By incorporating these criteria into the curriculum, the Art Matters Club provided a truly immersive and comprehensive learning experience.

Through the club, students had the opportunity to take on the role of being conservators and delve into various facets of art conservation while simultaneously forging connections with their cultural and environmental surroundings.

Program Content

The consistent format of the Art Matters Club, with its weekly sessions, was structured as follows:

Session 1: Becoming a Conservator

This first session introduced the fundamental concepts of art conservation and established a foundation for their learning journey. Students received their conservator kits (Figure 9.1). They were encouraged to carefully examine each tool, guided by the instructor's explanations. The students also prepared individual equipment boxes to store lab coats and kits after each session.

Session 2: Trick or Treat

The second session considered paper lightfastness, handling, and storage. Students looked at color differences before and after light exposure. Paper designs related to Halloween themes were cut out and taped on colorful paper and exposed to light for three weeks.

Sessions 3 and 4: Paper

The topic of the next two sessions was printing techniques on paper and support systems, exploring subtractive printing using thin blue sheets of

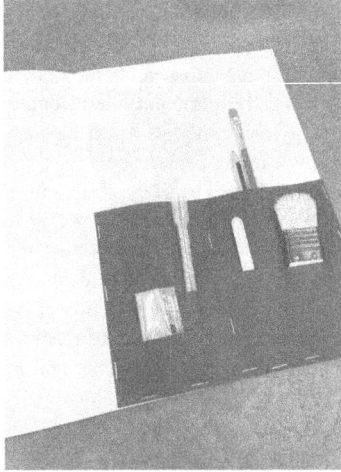

Figure 9.1 Conservator kit given to each student at the beginning of the program.
Photo by Raquel Santos.

Styrofoam for artistic purposes. The foam was carved with toothpicks or similar wooden tools, eliminating the need for knives or blades.

Sessions 5 and 6: Ceramics

The subject of glass and ceramic artworks and their differences was covered over two sessions. Students cleaned and reconstructed clay pots that were previously broken by the program instructor and individually set up for students to handle.

Sessions 7 and 8: Cold Treatment

The last two sessions of the club looked at sculptures and discovered how different mediums and materials respond to the environment. Students created their own sculptures using upcycled materials and exposed them to outdoor cold temperatures and low-light conditions typical of Norwegian winters.

Structure of Sessions

The program was carefully designed to provide a lively and captivating learning environment for students. Its primary goal was to foster critical thinking, creativity, and an appreciation for art conservation practices. Furthermore, it aimed to encourage a more profound level of engagement by promoting observation, exploration of materials and techniques, critical thinking, and creativity.

Each session commenced with a ten-to-fifteen-minute introduction, focusing on a specific topic. These thought-provoking conversations encouraged children to contemplate various artistic mediums found both in artworks and everyday life. To facilitate a more focused exploration of specific preservation requirements, virtual visits to museum galleries were organized, showcasing diverse artworks and collections.

In select sessions, students had the opportunity to embark on remote visits to conservation laboratories and studios, guided by conservators from institutions worldwide. This firsthand experience exposed students to artworks undergoing treatment and enabled interactions with specialists from different backgrounds. Through these interactive components, students developed a deeper understanding of art preservation.

Following these visits, age-appropriate hands-on activities were provided, allowing students to apply their newly acquired knowledge and develop practical skills. At the conclusion of each session, students were asked to complete a reflective questionnaire, simulating their own "artwork condition reports" (Figure 9.2). This exercise served to consolidate their learning and express their insights. The questionnaire, consisting of four carefully crafted questions, was designed to accommodate the participation of young students who were still in the process of developing their reading and writing skills.

92   *Raquel Santos*

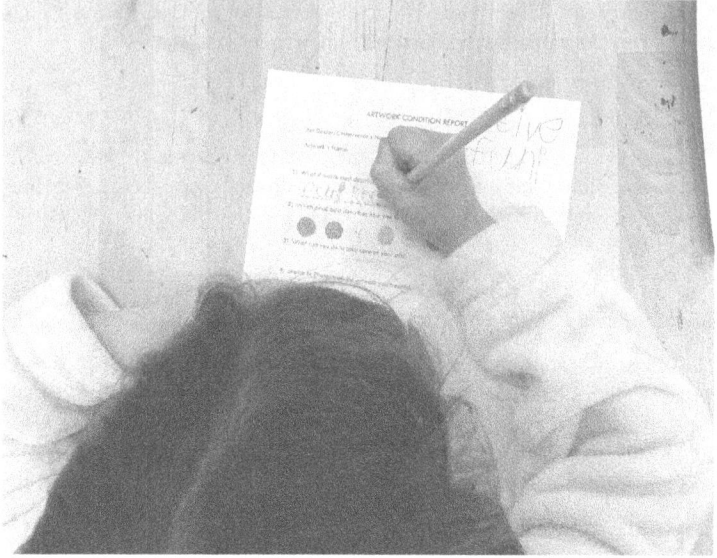

Figure 9.2 Student filling out an artwork condition report at the end of the hands-on activity.

Photo by Raquel Santos.

Feedback

The program received positive feedback from both parents and enrolled students, who were enthusiastic about the discoveries from each session. Overall, parents of children enrolled reported the following:

- They were thrilled to have an offering that provided cultural and intellectual richness, which is rare for this age group, especially in a small town.
- They appreciated that the class was taught by a conservator who not only was knowledgeable but also had a playful and artistic approach when working with children of this age group.
- They enjoyed the format of the program, which included hands-on activities and role-playing, as well as virtual interactions with other professionals to inspire the students.
- They acknowledged that while schools and preschools often emphasize the importance of conserving nature from a young age, it was great to see the program expand on that by teaching young children about appreciating and preserving human heritage.
- They observed that the children were enthusiastic about reflecting on art conservation beyond the classroom and actively engaging and questioning the care of artworks around them.

The program generally received positive reviews from both parents and students, with parents expressing their excitement about the unique offering and its impact on their children's cultural and intellectual development. Furthermore, parents of older PYP students at the school approached to inquire about the possibility of enrolling their children in future editions of the club.

Key Takeaways and Potential Enhancements

Throughout the program, students immersed themselves in various conservation techniques and tools, gaining a comprehensive understanding of the intricacies and practices involved in conservation efforts. The original design of the program allocated only forty-five minutes per session, with each session focusing on a different topic. However, it became evident that students needed more time and support to fully engage in and complete activities. As a result, the program was modified to dedicate two forty-five-minute sessions to a single topic, employing a building-up system where the concepts introduced in each session laid the foundation for the understanding of the next, enabling more in-depth exploration as outlined in the Program Content section.

Moreover, the opportunity for semester-long engagement had a significant impact on what students derived from the program. With an extended duration for each topic, students had the opportunity to delve deeper into the subject matter, develop a stronger grasp of the concepts, and apply their knowledge in practical scenarios. The longer timeframe facilitated a more comprehensive understanding, while also fostering curiosity, reflection, and active participation, ultimately enhancing the overall learning experience for the students. Active participation from students was observed during hands-on activities, along with their willingness to share thoughts and ask questions. This interactive approach sparked curiosity and facilitated meaningful connections between concepts and personal experiences.

The program not only helped students develop critical thinking and problem-solving skills but also raised awareness among caregivers about the significance of art conservation. In future interactions, it would be beneficial to involve caregivers in at least one of the hands-on activities. By incorporating caregivers into the program, we could create an opportunity for them to actively engage with their children and deepen their understanding of art conservation together. This involvement not only fosters a stronger connection between caregivers and children but also allows parents to become advocates for art conservation and reinforce the importance of preserving cultural heritage.

Including caregivers in a hands-on activity provides a platform for collaborative learning and promotes a shared experience that can be carried beyond the program itself. Caregivers can contribute their unique perspectives and knowledge, enriching the learning environment for both the children and adults. Additionally, it encourages open communication and dialogue, facilitating the exchange of ideas and reflections on the significance of art conservation. By incorporating caregiver participation into the hands-on activities, the program not only extends its impact beyond the classroom but also empowers families to become active participants in preserving and appreciating art.

Integrating art conservation into the PYP curriculum proved to be an effective means of engaging children in learning about cultural heritage preservation. The success of integrating art conservation into the PYP curriculum highlights the potential for similar approaches to be equally effective and worthwhile in non-IB education systems. By adopting age-appropriate programs with hands-on activities and interactive learning, schools outside the IB framework can also foster a genuine understanding and appreciation for art conservation among young learners. Emphasizing the value of preserving cultural heritage and artistic expressions can be a universally beneficial aspect of any educational curriculum, regardless of the educational framework.

Additionally, integrating art conservation into non-IB curricula can offer a rich opportunity to blend art with science and social studies, promoting cross-disciplinary learning. It can empower students to explore not only the technical aspects of conservation but also the historical and cultural contexts of artworks and artifacts. By encouraging active engagement in preservation efforts, students can develop a sense of responsibility and empathy toward their cultural heritage, instilling a lifelong commitment to protecting and cherishing artistic treasures.

Furthermore, art conservation education can cultivate critical thinking and problem-solving skills as students encounter real-world challenges in preserving and restoring artworks. Encouraging creativity and innovation in conservation methods can be a valuable addition to any education system, nurturing students' ability to approach complex issues with ingenuity and resourcefulness.

In conclusion, incorporating art conservation into non-IB education systems can offer numerous benefits, including fostering a deeper connection with art, promoting cross-disciplinary learning, instilling a sense of cultural responsibility, and nurturing critical thinking skills. These outcomes can contribute to well-rounded and culturally aware individuals who appreciate and actively contribute to the preservation of their artistic heritage.

Acknowledgments

Enormous gratitude goes to my Smithsonian colleagues, in particular Ellen Chase and Jenifer Bosworth, for their inspiration and unwavering support. I also extend my heartfelt thanks to Gjøvikregionen International School, caregivers, and students for believing in and supporting this project. Their collective commitment has made it possible to integrate conservation outreach into our International Baccalaureate, Primary Years Program's after-school activities, creating an environment where art and conservation intersect to enhance our educational journey.

Biography

Raquel Santos, an art educator at Gjøvikregionen International School in Norway, offers significant expertise in textile preservation and curation as a trained art conservator. Her contributions have benefited institutions in the United States, Portugal, and Switzerland. From 2011 to 2021, Raquel played a vital role in establishing and managing a research project at the Centre for Humanities, NOVA University of Lisbon, Portugal, with a focus on enhancing awareness of the artistic and historical importance of textiles. Committed to advancing art knowledge and preservation, she emphasizes utilizing art's educational potential in diverse settings, including museums, schools, and public spaces. Raquel is dedicated to crafting meaningful learning experiences, nurturing cross-disciplinary art, and cultural heritage appreciation.

References

IBO (International Baccalaureate Organization). n.d. "Primary Years Programme." Accessed April 9, 2023. https://www.ibo.org/programmes/primary-years-programme/.
———. 2018. *Primary Years Programme, Learning and Teaching*. Cardiff, United Kingdom: IBO.

10 School Community Partnerships

Developing STEAM Resources about Cultural Heritage Preservation

Renée Stein

Introduction

In my role as the Director of Conservation at the Michael C. Carlos Museum, I initiated the department's STEAM (Science, Technology, Engineering, Art, Mathematics) resources for school children from kindergarten through fifth grade (aged five to ten). I began where I had ready access: at our neighborhood elementary school with my own children's classes, offering to bring enrichment activities connecting art and science. Concurrently, the school was seeking community partners in its initiative to incorporate innovative, interdisciplinary instruction into curricula. As my children advanced, teachers and volunteers helped develop grade-appropriate, curriculum-connected learning activities. At each level, we identified science topics that relate to the work of preserving tangible cultural heritage. Some topics focused on materials, while other topics linked to preventive care. Examples of art objects and preservation actions were drawn from the Carlos Museum. Through these classroom activities, we aimed to foster a relationship between the museum and the school community of teachers, students, and families.

Partners

The School

Like all partnerships, this relationship is defined by the characteristics and resources of its participants. Briarlake Elementary School (BES) is a public school in the Dekalb County School District in metro-Atlanta, Georgia, a diverse system that serves more than 90,000 students and includes over 14,000 employees. It is important to note that BES is a publicly funded school with supplementary resources, as opposed to a tuition-based private school. BES enrolls 385 to 425 children in grades pre-kindergarten through fifth grade (aged four to ten) and employs approximately eighty staff. In this district,

DOI: 10.4324/9781003333210-12

children generally attend elementary schools near their residences, and the BES neighborhood zone is less than four square miles. The student population is diverse with a white majority of less than 40%. The school prides itself on strong relationships with the community and offers an array of extracurricular opportunities that are supported by teachers, administrators, and parents.

BES received its first STEM (Science, Technology, Engineering, Mathematics) certification in 2017, recognizing its school-wide program to pilot new, interdisciplinary lesson plans augmented by business and community partnerships, including this collaboration with the Carlos Museum's Conservation Department. The program aims to embed STEM instructional practices in all classrooms across all grade levels. These student-centered learning strategies use problem-based learning, investigation, and inquiry to foster communication, critical thinking, and creativity. STEAM incorporates art as a complementary subject that employs these same instructional practices and learning strategies. Art conservation engages both art and science, exemplifying many principles of STEAM instruction.

The Museum

The Michael C. Carlos Museum is located on the campus of Emory University, approximately five miles from BES. Emory is a private university that includes an undergraduate college and seven professional schools. The museum collections include art and artifacts from Africa; ancient Egypt, Nubia, and the Near East; ancient Greece and Rome; the Indigenous Americas; and South Asia; as well as American and European works on paper. The staff of approximately thirty-five includes two staff conservators, one grant-funded post-graduate fellow, contract specialists, and student interns who are exploring heritage preservation careers. Conservators collaborate with other staff to accomplish both long-term preventive care and more immediate interventive treatment of the collections. The Conservation Department has a long-standing commitment to raising awareness about and promoting access to cultural heritage preservation through classes and internships as well as public programming.

Activities

We developed activities for two grade levels each year for three years, beginning with kindergarten and fourth grade. Learning objectives for each grade level are outlined within the Georgia Performance Standards or the Georgia Standards of Excellence. In some cases, lesson plans aligned to both standards. The activities provide guidelines for content as well as instruction and assessment. Reviewing these standards, we identified intersections between the topics presented at each grade level and practices for the preservation of cultural heritage. Conservators devised the activities, which were revised and refined with input from teachers and students. In most cases, conservators brought supplies into classrooms and led the activities, gathering observations and feedback.

We created activities that pair with at least one standard for science education and may also connect to other curricular topics, including math, geography, history, and art. According to the Georgia Standards of Excellence, students will "obtain, evaluate, and communicate" information or observations about topics (Georgia Department of Education 2023). There are a variety of ways students can fulfill this requirement, including conducting investigations, engaging the senses, using tools, collecting data, recognizing patterns, and compiling records. Activities complement these learning goals. Some activities include artmaking. Each activity includes examples from the Carlos Museum's collection or its preservation procedures.

- Kindergarten (age five) students learn about *bogolanfini* (mudcloth) from Mali, Africa, and design their own cloths. As part of a science unit on soil, they collect soil to make mud paint, create patterns on cloth with shape stickers, and apply the mud paint with sponges. They observe the colors and textures of the mud paint. They also sort and count shapes, measure their cloth, and record information on worksheets.
- First-grade (age six to seven) students test the strength of different types of magnets and apply this knowledge to mounting art materials, such as paper, cloth, felt, and cardboard. They measure material samples and assess the comparative weights by feel. Students evaluate the strength of different magnets, predict which will be needed for each material, and then test their hypotheses, recording observations on worksheets.
- Second-grade (age seven to eight) students compare physical changes of stone, clay, and wax due to water or heat. They record observations on a worksheet and complete a comparison "double-bubble" thinking chart. They learn how ancient Egyptians used these materials and how art conservators use wax to protect and repair objects. Based on their hands-on learning, students theorize why an ancient stone vessel leaned to one side while on display in the museum. They also have the opportunity to create a wax mask.
- Third-grade (age eight to nine) students investigate the physical properties of a variety of rocks and minerals, including color, texture, luster, hardness, and streak. They consider how these attributes can be chosen and manipulated for specific uses. They match vocabulary with definitions, record observations on a worksheet, and create a bubble map of characteristics for specific rocks or minerals. Students learn about ancient stone-working for sculpture, building, tools, and jewelry. On the basis of physical attributes, they pair rocks and minerals with these uses, explain their reasoning, and exchange information with classmates.

- Fourth-grade (age nine to ten) students measure the intensity of light through opaque, translucent, and transparent materials. They match vocabulary to definitions and graph intensity data on a worksheet. They also compare the energy usage of incandescent, fluorescent, and LED bulbs. They select one bulb type and calculate the cost to light a gallery with many lamps. They share data to compare and choose a cost-effective bulb. Students may also make art using light-sensitive papers and sunlight.

- Fifth-grade (age ten to eleven) students experiment with magnetic systems and observe how the thickness of a material being hung by a magnet affects the strength of the system. They learn about ways magnets are used in museums to mount artwork on display or to hold pieces together during repair. Students record measurements, weights, and experimental observations on a worksheet. They graph data and describe whether the decrease in strength is linear or exponential.

A short presentation accompanies each activity to communicate central themes and introduce assignment steps before students work individually or in small groups. Images of objects from the Carlos Museum's collection are featured in these presentations, making connections between the activity, cultural heritage, and preservation. Presentations afford additional opportunities to connect with curriculum standards, such as using maps or learning about careers.

For example, kindergarten students see images of mudcloth, including an example in the Carlos Museum. They also locate Mali on a map of Africa and view images of other objects from Mali in the museum's collection. After making mudcloth, they may read *The Magic Gourd: A West African Folktale* by Baba Wagué Diakité, whose illustrations include patterns recalling mudcloth designs. Some presentations introduce the work of preservation professionals, demonstrating how magnets are used in display or repair and how materials are identified by careful evaluation of their physical properties.

Collaborators

Teachers welcomed us into their classrooms to test out activities and offered feedback about developmental appropriateness and curricular relevance along with suggestions for revision. Each grade level had a lead science teacher, who was the point of contact for our collaboration. These teachers coordinated across the grade so that activities could occur in all classes on one day, often simultaneously or in consecutive rotation. Teachers were present to provide classroom management and also to assist students with the activities. They experienced the activities alongside the students and made suggestions to improve learning outcomes or connect with adjacent curricula. For example, a first-grade teacher suggested that students should handle the magnets informally to become familiar with how they behaved before beginning the assignment to compare the relative strengths. The fourth-grade social studies teacher offered pertinent topics from American history that could resonate through highlight objects, such as Harriet Tubman's shawl, Abraham Lincoln's hat, and Sitting Bull's feather headdress.

University students, conservation interns, and museum volunteers were essential to the development and execution of the activities. They helped plan experiments, prepare supplies, and conduct activities in elementary school classes. A physics major interested in education created the magnets activities as a project for university academic credit. He came to BES to guide the fifth-grade activity and made adjustments to his worksheet and presentation based on observations from the students and teachers. A graduate conservation intern with prior experience as a science teacher developed the second-grade activity on physical properties of matter and the third-grade activity on rocks. A retired teacher and volunteer museum docent helped prepare supplies and instruct kindergarten students in making mudcloth. Her grandchildren attended the school, and she became a passionate advocate for this partnership.

After the initial year of running an activity at a grade level, teachers intended to lead the activity in their classes using the provided resources, including the classroom presentations, notes, and worksheets. In the first several years of the partnership, I attended meetings of the science teachers to provide an overview of the program and meet teachers from the next grade level with whom I would create more activities. The school added STEM to the rotation of "specials," along with music, art, and physical education. They hired a STEM teacher, who incorporated the museum activities into her classes. She generously brought expertise, creativity, and enthusiasm to the partnership, and she worked closely with the conservation graduate intern to prepare teacher guides for the activities.

Educator Resources

To ensure the sustainability of this initiative, I needed to shift from what I could do directly to what teachers could implement on their own to meet the needs of their classes. Making the activities accessible to teachers would also mean that the materials could be used at other schools. The COVID-19 pandemic accelerated the need for ready-made resources for teachers, and limitations on classroom access forced the transition. During the year and a half of remote and hybrid classes, we worked to create a website for the kindergarten through fifth grade activities and associated resources. We created a Scholarblog site, which is the Wordpress platform supported by Emory University and tied to my faculty profile (Figure 10.1). Distinct from the museum's website, the K-5 Art & Science Activities site will not be impacted by future revisions and can be updated by conservation staff (Carlos Museum n.d.).

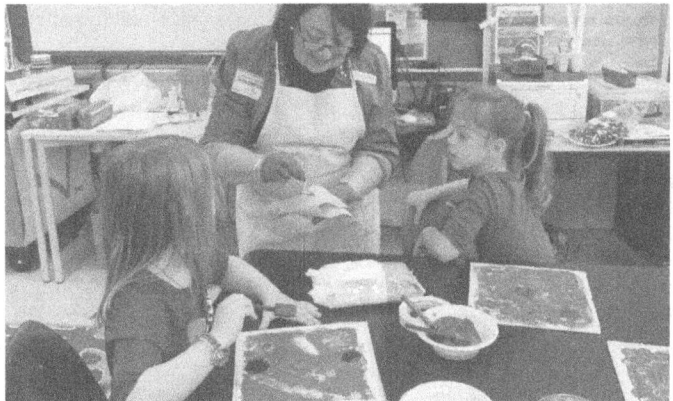

K-5 Art & Science Activities

STEAM lab activities focus on art materials and conservation practices. Developed in partnership with experienced classroom teachers and STEAM educators, activities are paired with Georgia and National Performance Standards for elementary education. Resources include teacher guides, student worksheets, and class presentations.

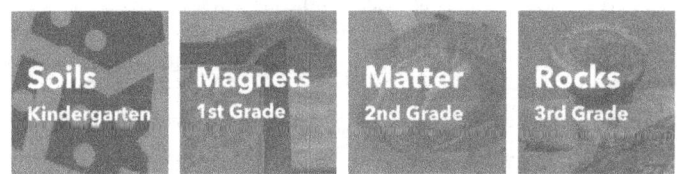

Figure 10.1 Landing page for K-5 Art & Science Activities website.
Photo by Veena Black.

During the pandemic, a conservation graduate intern converted the resources to a lesson plan template provided by the museum's Education Department. The STEM teacher reviewed these lesson plans, which became teacher guides for each activity. The graduate intern produced illustrated how-to notes to help teachers visualize the activities, including supplies and procedures. She created classroom presentations that provide pacing and include presentation notes. Each activity also has a student worksheet. All of these materials are individual PDFs that open in separate browser windows and can be downloaded.

A team of five undergraduates formatted these materials on the Scholarblog site. Paid through an existing grant from the Andrew W. Mellon Foundation, these students worked remotely during the summer, meeting with me weekly over video conference and meeting in person once to stage photographs for the website. These students chose the website layout with a landing page and tiles as well as drop-down menus leading to each activity by topic and grade level. Each activity page features learning objectives and guiding questions, along with relevant national and Georgia education standards. The teacher guide, how-to notes, student worksheet, classroom presentation, and presentation notes PDFs are linked via consistent icons on each activity page. The activity pages also include three captioned images that provide a visual preview of the content. The K-5 Art & Science Activities website is linked to the Conservation Resources webpage of the Carlos Museum's website.

Looking Ahead

Students and teachers returned to the classrooms in spring or fall 2021. However, volunteer access and field-trip restrictions extended into the following school year. I communicated with teachers through email, writing directly to science leads and providing links to the new website. I loaned supplies for the activities, and the dedicated volunteer prepared materials at home, dropping them off for classroom use. During this time, several teachers and administrators changed roles or moved away from BES. Less than 25% of the current staff were present when the museum partnership was first established in 2017. The school continues its STEM emphasis but phased out the STEM "special," and the STEM lead teacher has since returned to a grade-level classroom. She and several other teachers continue to use some of the activities we developed. When field trips resumed in the 2022 to 2023 academic year, both the second and fourth grades visited the Carlos Museum. When the fourth grade toured, they specifically requested to see examples of how the museum addresses concerns related to light exposure, which is the fourth-grade activity topic. Conservators provided information to docents about materials that are vulnerable to light damage and preventive care methods to mitigate exposure, including the use of LED bulbs and motion-activated lights, as well as the short-term display of sensitive objects at lower light levels.

My original vision for this program was that every BES student would encounter the Carlos Museum and cultural heritage preservation through the STEAM activities at each grade level. I hoped that every student would experience at least one field trip to the museum and that their families would become familiar with its programming. This cumulative exposure would foster an awareness of cultural heritage preservation and conservation practice, as well as an understanding that museums and collections are resources for interdisciplinary teaching and learning. I hoped that the STEM lead teacher would share the resources we developed at BES with her colleagues throughout the school district. This ambitious vision seemed attainable, beginning on a local level and small scale. Despite disruptions in the continuity of both process and participants, the desired impact may yet be realized although at a slower pace and more modest scope than originally imagined.

Making conservation accessible to students and public audiences remains a priority for the Carlos Museum's Conservation Department, and it is intentionally integrated into projects, internships, and funding opportunities. Working with younger audiences requires that we identify an appropriate intersection, in this case the curricular objectives for each grade level, and that we seek guidance on how to communicate effectively. Teachers and students offered valuable suggestions to make activities more relevant and useful. Undergraduate students and emerging conservators were essential contributors who also gained experience with community engagement.

Partnerships are built upon relationships, requiring time, commitment, and investment.

The personal relationships that originally fostered this partnership and the momentum to promote the activities have shifted. Ultimately, providing these activities is not the primary responsibility of either the conservation staff or the teachers with whom we initially collaborated. This reality necessitated that we transition our resources online where we hope that they will be discovered, used, and shared. The activities may also evolve and be utilized in new ways. The Carlos Museum offers conservation tours, which highlight examples of treatment, preventive care, and research. These tours are led by docents in the galleries or facilitated by museum educators in an interactive virtual version. Although typically offered for fourth grade and above, docents frequently incorporate conservation information into tours for all ages, often matching examples to topics identified by teachers.

The online STEAM activities pair well with these tours, providing complementary resources for teachers and students to engage with conservation-related themes of materials and preventive care. Museum educators and conservators are exploring ways to incorporate these STEAM activities into future teacher workshops and summer camps. Fostering learning about and appreciation for the art and science of conservation is an important means to make cultural heritage preservation a shared priority in our global society.

Acknowledgments

This comprehensive, multi-year initiative would not have been possible without the tremendous contributions of STEM teacher Veena Black and former graduate intern, Objects Conservator Elena Bowen. The teachers, administrators, and students of Briarlake Elementary School were important partners. Other contributors include Assistant Conservator Brittany Dinneen, Professor Connie Roth, Conservation Fellow Jessica Betz Abel, conservation interns Clara Gonzales and Michaela Paulson, and as well as undergraduate students Audra Buffington, Benjamin Kasavan, Payton Malone, Kayla Moorhead, Aron Sohn, and Jeffrey Yang. Volunteer Christine Brandes continues to provide invigorating enthusiasm.

Biography

Renée Stein is Director of Conservation at the Michael C. Carlos Museum at Emory University in Atlanta, GA. She oversees the treatment, preventive care, and technical analysis of the varied collections. Stein is also an Associate Teaching Professor in the Art History Department, offering courses on conservation and technical study. She is a Fellow of the American Institute for Conservation of Historic and Artistic Works, and her career has been shaped by a commitment to outreach, fostering education about and encouraging appreciation for cultural heritage preservation among all ages.

References

Georgia Department of Education. 2023. "Science Georgia Standards of Excellence (GSE) K-5." Accessed 30 September, 2023. https://www.georgiastandards.org/Georgia-Standards/Pages/Science-K-5.aspx.

Michael C. Carlos Museum, Emory University. 2023. "K-5 Art & Science Activities." Accessed 30 September, 2023. https://scholarblogs.emory.edu/k-5steamactivities/.

Conclusion

Ellen Chase, Laura Hoffman,
and Matthew Lasnoski

Throughout the course of this book, we have looked at the value of cultural heritage preservation outreach for early learners, a number of possible approaches and manners to carry that out, and the tools to evaluate the outreach, both to create more effective programming and to show its benefits. While there are still far fewer conservation programs for early learners than for other ages, the amount of outreach targeted for this group has grown since we started this journey back in 2016, and there is certainly room for more development. We hope that the book has given a sense of the importance of such programming, whether virtual or in-person, and some insight into potential ways to begin this type of engagement.

The Diverse Landscape of Early Learner Outreach

The Smithsonian's Art & Me program, along with the case studies featured in Part II, demonstrates multiple ways meaningful conservation outreach programs can be crafted for early learners. The programs showcase the versatility of approaches tailored to the size of the institution, target age group, and available resources. This range of approaches highlights that there is no one-size-fits-all method for engaging young children in cultural heritage conservation. From museum programs with after school centers to independently led activity days for intergenerational audiences, successful early learner programs can take many forms. We hope that these real-world examples will encourage future outreach and engagement programs, as well as lead the way for others to generate new models, including more self-guided models like exhibitions and online resources for early learners.

Collaboration and Innovation

Bring Professionals Together

While collaboration between conservators and educators is an ideal approach for early learning outreach, we recognize that not everyone has easy

DOI: 10.4324/9781003333210-13

access to such interaction. However, since both professions are generous with their interests and knowledge, we hope this book inspires individuals to think innovatively about how to bring conservators and educators together. Whether it is a conservator reaching out to teachers at a local school, such as the school community partnership between the Michael C. Carlos Museum and Briarlake Elementary, or an educator reaching out to conservators at a museum or professional organization, various avenues for collaboration can lead to engaging programming for early learners that builds on expertise from both fields.

Adapting Existing Programs and Utilizing Available Resources

While developing programs from the ground up is certainly possible, as we did with the Art & Me program, it is equally feasible to adapt existing programs for older children to suit early learners or to adapt a nonconservation early learning program. Underlying structures and knowledge of an existing program can provide a solid foundation for a program, potentially reducing the initial investment of time and resources. The Cleveland Museum of Art's adaptation of the Art to Go program for early learners shows how a fully developed program for older children can be extended to this younger audience. Equally, programming can be done with a range of budgets or can capitalize on existing offerings in this respect as well. Programs do not have to break the bank; innovation can happen by making use of available resources in new ways.

Key Considerations for Success

Identifying Target Audiences and Establishing Goals

One of the first critical steps is defining a target audience and establishing clear program goals. When working with early learners, there are many considerations: should the engagement focus on young children in a formal or informal learning environment? Will the program be developed with a K-12 teacher for their students in a classroom setting or in the museum? For intergenerational programming, how can the content be scaled up for multiple ages and engage caregivers? Identifying the audience and program objectives are essential for success.

From our example with the Art & Me program, we learned that program goals should be long term and achievable. Those looking to develop their own conservation outreach programming may want to consider the specific program objectives and learning outcomes. The overarching Art & Me program goal is learning the foundations and importance of cultural heritage preservation through conservation storytelling and artmaking. Without establishing well-defined learning outcomes, it becomes challenging to assess a program's effectiveness.

Listening to the Audience

The evolving needs of a target audience guide program development. Regularly collecting data for comparison purposes and using consistent metrics over time are crucial for program evaluation. Those embarking on evaluating a program should focus on collecting data that aligns with program objectives and does not overwhelm participants. For the Art & Me program team, we focus on short, targeted surveys that focus on the participant experience since caregivers have limited time.

Developing a Program Structure and Content

In embarking on a new program, one should consider the goals and audience to design an age-appropriate and cohesive structure. The Art Matters Club was developed as a new program with the goal of supplementing an IB curriculum, which has a very different aim than a more informal one-day event. Structure and content are key whether the program is new or adapted. Developing content for a pre-existing structure may involve testing out activities, materials, and the overall timing and flow, as demonstrated by the American University of Beirut Archaeological Museum. It is equally important to consider the program topic and how the structure can support the learning outcomes, which will likely evolve over time.

Sustainability and Program Frequency

When considering the sustainability and frequency of a new program, it is important to think through how this program can be offered without putting too much strain on resources. First and foremost, starting small can be a smart and strategic decision for initiating a program. There are many models from a one-time offering, such as the *Haf o Hwyl* conservation activity day, to an ongoing series, like the Heritage Conservation Centre's Little Conservators program. Establishing key players early on is vital not only in getting a program off the ground but also in supporting this program over time. A great deal of the Art & Me success has been the sustained collaboration of conservators and educators. For many, generating revenue may be a priority and an institutional goal for any new approved programming. If so, the structure of the program should fit into a revenue-based model, such as youth camps. In other situations, covering costs may be more of a necessity than generating income to foster institutional buy-in, in which case it is important to create a budget and a paid registration-based model for the program.

Inspiring Change: Building a Bright Future for Cultural Heritage Preservation

Stakeholder Engagement

By clearly communicating the program outcomes, one can identify key stakeholders to champion the program and build institutional support. The right partners can utilize their skills to build a collaborative program that is far richer in content and facilitation. With all of these factors in place, innovative programs can help build a new generation of young learners who will appreciate the importance of cultural heritage preservation, and possibly, future conservators.

Long-Term Sustainability

The long-term sustainability of cultural heritage conservation and research depends on the support of the communities in which it exists and active engagement with those communities. We hope this book has shown that beginning these interactions with young children is less intimidating than it might seem and can only strengthen these connections that are so essential to preserving world heritage. Plus, collaborating to create the Art & Me program has been an incredibly fun and rewarding experience that we would encourage others to try.

The path to preserving our cultural heritage is a shared journey. We hope this book has equipped readers with insights, inspiration, and practical guidance to embark on a mission to bridge the past with the future, one early learner at a time.

Appendix A

Questionnaire

Ellen Chase, Laura Hoffman,
and Matthew Lasnoski

Overview

From October 2019 to April 2023, there have been four survey versions administered to evaluate the Art & Me program:

Onsite NMAA Public Programs Survey (October 2019 to March 2020)

The Audience Research Team (ART) planned a yearlong study of all public programs at the National Museum of Asian Art (NMAA). The Art & Me program was included as one of the programs that would be surveyed. Due to the COVID-19 pandemic, this version of the survey ended in March 2020 and a new survey was developed for programs that would be offered online. There are twelve Art & Me program surveys collected in this version.

Onsite SAAM Lunder Conservation Outreach Survey (Fall 2019)

The Smithsonian American Art Museum's (SAAM) Lunder Conservation Center joined the Art & Me program in 2019 and started to pilot onsite programs. Prior to the COVID-19 pandemic, the Lunder Conservation Center offered one Art & Me workshop two times onsite at SAAM. In this workshop, they collected eight completed surveys from the Art & Me workshop.

Online NMAA Public Programs Survey (March 2020 to September 2020)

In response to the COVID-19 pandemic, NMAA created an updated version of the yearlong Public Programs survey. The survey was shortened, and several questions were updated to reflect experiences unique to the online format. There are eighteen Art & Me program surveys collected in this version from the first two online joint NMAA and SAAM Art & Me workshops.

Online Art & Me Survey (October 2020 to April 2023)

Once the NMAA Public Programs survey concluded, the Art & Me program team continued to evaluate its workshops. The survey used many standard questions from previous NMAA survey questions but customized several questions for their audience and utilized questions from the SAAM survey. This survey version comprises 112 of the 150 Art & Me survey responses.

In Appendix A, readers are provided with the questions of two versions of the Art & Me survey: the Onsite NMAA Public Programs Survey and the Online Art & Me Survey. The intention behind sharing these versions of the survey is to provide examples of potential surveys for onsite and online conservation outreach programs.

Onsite NMAA Public Programs Survey (October 2019 to March 2020)

Is this your first visit to the National Museum of Asian Art?

• No
• Yes

Display if Yes to Is this your first visit to the National Museum of Asian Art

How many times have you visited the National Museum of Asian Art in the past twelve months?

• 0
• 1
• 2 to 3
• 4 to 10
• 10 or more

Please rate your overall experience at this program today.

• Poor
• Fair
• Good
• Excellent
• Superior

Did you come to the museum today specifically to attend this program?

- No
- Yes

Where did you hear about this event? (Mark one or more)

- Word of mouth (family, friend, hotel concierge, etc.)
- Advertisement (newspaper, magazine, radio, online, etc.)
- News story (newspaper, magazine, radio, online, etc.)
- Smithsonian or National Museum of Asian Art website, calendar, or e-newsletter
- Information desk at National Museum of Asian Art or other Smithsonian museum
- Social media (Facebook, Twitter, blog, etc.)
- None of these, I wandered by
- Other

Display if Other to Where did you hear about this event? (Mark or more)

Where did you hear about this program?

Did anything in this program surprise you?

- No
- Yes

Display if Yes to Did anything in this program surprise you?

What surprised you?

Which factors were the most satisfying in your visit today? (Mark one or more)

- To have fun and be entertained
- To learn something new or feel intellectually stimulated
- To socialize or be with friends and family
- To relax and slow down
- To feel inspired or admire things that are beautiful or interesting

- To have a new experience (by visiting a museum of exhibition I haven't seen)
- To give friends or family an enjoyable experience
- None of the above

How interested are you in the following?

Asian art

- Not/Slightly interested
- Somewhat interested
- Interested
- Very interested

Asian history/culture

- Not/slightly interested
- Somewhat interested
- Interested
- Very interested

What is your age?

- 18 to 19
- 20 to 24
- 25 to 29
- 30 to 34
- 35 to 39
- 40 to 44
- 45 to 49
- 50 to 54
- 55 to 59
- 60 to 64
- 65 to 69
- 70 and over

Who are you visiting with today? (Mark one or more)

- I am alone
- One or more adults
- One or more youth under 18

With what gender do you identify?

- Female
- Male
- Non-binary
- Transgender
- Other
- Prefer not to specify

Display if Other to With what gender do you identify?

Please specify your gender identification.

Where do you live?

- United States
- Another country

Display if United States to Where do you live?

Please specify zip code.

Display if Another country to Where do you live?

Please specify country.

Please select the background(s) with which you most identify. Select as many as apply.

- African American or Black
- Native American or Alaskan Native
- Asian (Chinese, Indian, Vietnamese, Filipino/a, etc.)

- Caucasian and White
- Hispanic, Latino, or Spanish
- Middle Eastern or North African
- Native Hawaiian or Other Pacific Islander
- I do not see myself in this list provided
- Prefer not to specify

Display if I do not see myself in this list provided to Please select your background(s) with which you most identify. Select as many as apply.

With what background do you most identify?

_____

What would you like to tell us about your overall experience?

_____

Online Art & Me Survey (October 2020 to April 2023)

Is this your first time attending an online program with the National Museum of Asian Art and/or Smithsonian American Art Museum?

- Yes
- No

Display if No to Is this your first time attending an online program with the National Museum of Asian Art and/or Smithsonian American Art Museum?

Is this your first time attending an Art & Me Family Preservation workshop?

- Yes
- No

Display if No to Is this your first time attending an Art & Me Family Preservation workshop?

What motivated you to attend more than one Art & Me program?

_____

Please rate your overall experience at this program today.

- Poor
- Fair

- Good
- Excellent
- Outstanding

Which factors were the most satisfying today? (Mark one or more)

- To have fun or be entertained
- To learn something new or feel intellectually
- To socialize or be with friends and family
- To relax and slow down
- To feel inspired or admire things that are beautiful or interesting
- To have a new experience (by cultural program online)
- To give friends of family an enjoyable experience
- None of the above

Did anything in the program surprise you?

- No
- Yes

Display if Yes to Did anything in the program surprise you?

What surprised you?

Where did you hear about this program? (Mark one or more)

When did you hear about this program? (Mark one or more)

- Smithsonian museum website (asia.si.edu or americanart.si.edu)
- Word of mouth (family, friend, hotel, concierge, etc.)
- Advertisement or sponsored post (print or digital)
- News story/article (newspaper, magazine, radio, online, etc.)
- Online event or activity listing (Eventbrite, things to do, etc.)
- Smithsonian museum print and/or e-newsletter
- Social media (Facebook, Twitter, or Instagram)
- Other

Display if Other to When did you hear about this program?

Where did you hear about this online program?

What is your age?

- 18 to 19
- 20 to 24
- 25 to 29
- 30 to 34
- 35 to 39
- 40 to 44
- 45 to 49
- 50 to 54
- 55 to 59
- 60 to 64
- 65 to 69
- 70 and over

Where do you live?

- United States
- Another country

Display if United States to Where do you live?

Please specify zip code.

Display if Another country to Where do you live?

Please specify country.

Please select the background(s) with which you most identify. Select as many as apply.

- African American or Black
- Native American or Alaskan Native
- Asian (Chinese, Indian, Vietnamese, Filipino/a, etc.)
- Caucasian and White
- Hispanic, Latino, or Spanish

- Middle Eastern or North African
- Native Hawaiian or Other Pacific Islander
- I do not see myself in this list provided
- Prefer not to specify

Display if I do not see myself in this list provided to Please select your background(s) with which you most identify. Select as many as apply.

With what background do you most identify?

_____

What three words would you use to describe today's program?

_____

What other types of online programs would you like us to offer?

_____

Please share any additional comments about your overall experience today.

Appendix B
Survey Frequencies

*Ellen Chase, Laura Hoffman,
and Matthew Lasnoski*

Survey Results

*From the authors: Percentages may not sum to 100% due to rounding or
respondents' ability to select more than one response option. Survey frequen-
cies are only included for questions that appeared in all four survey versions
to ensure an appropriate sample size. Unless otherwise noted, the figures are
overall results across all survey versions.*

Number of survey responses: 150 surveys

Visitor Experience

Please rate your overall experience at this program today. (n = 150)

- Poor = 1%
- Fair = 0%
- Good = 10%
- Excellent = 39%
- Outstanding = 50%

Which factors were the most satisfying today? Mark one or more. (n = 150)

- To have fun or be entertained:
  - Yes = 59%
  - No = 41%
- To learn something new or feel intellectually stimulated:
  - Yes = 68%
  - No = 32%
- To socialize or be with friends and family:
  - Yes = 15%
  - No = 85%

- To relax and slow down:

  - Yes = 15%
  - No = 85%

- To feel inspired or admire things that are beautiful and interesting:

  - Yes = 56%
  - No = 44%

- To have a new experience (by a cultural program online):

  - Yes = 59%
  - No = 41%

- To give friends or family an enjoyable experience:

  - Yes = 51%
  - No = 49%

- None of the above:

  - Yes = 1%
  - No = 99%

Did anything in the program surprise you? (n = 124)

- Yes = 54%
- No = 46%

Visitor Context

What is your age? (n = 148)

- 18 to 19 = 3%
- 20 to 24 = 1%
- 25 to 29 = 1%
- 30 to 34 = 8%
- 35 to 39 = 23%
- 40 to 44 = 28%
- 45 to 49 = 6%
- 50 to 54 = 5%
- 55 to 59 = 3%
- 60 to 64 = 2%
- 65 to 69 = 12%
- 70 and over = 6%

Where do you live? *(n = 142)*

- United States = 89%
- Other Country = 11%

From the authors: Data for the following two questions are taken exclusively from the Online Art & Me survey version. Questions were modified between versions and cannot be combined.

Is this your first time attending an online program with the National Museum of Asian Art and/or Smithsonian American Art Museum? *(n = 114)*

- Yes = 55%
- No = 45%

How did you hear about this program? Mark one or more. *(n = 114)*

- Smithsonian museum website (asia.si.edu or americanart.si.edu) = 22%
- Word of mouth (family, friend, hotel, conceirge, etc.) = 20%
- Advertisement or sponsored post (print or digital) = 5%
- News story/article (newspaper, magazine, radio, online, etc.) = 8%
- Online event or activity listing (Eventbrite, things to do, etc.) = 36%
- Smithsonian museum print and/or e-newsletter = 22%
- Social media (Facebook, Twitter, or Instagram) = 14%
- Other = 4%

Index